THE ULTIMATE GUIDE ☆ ☆ ☆

TO GETTING YOUR GREEN CARD

LEARNINGEXPRESS®

NEW YORK

Library of Congress Cataloging-in-Publication Data
The ultimate guide to getting your green card.—1st ed.
  p.   cm.
  ISBN-13: 978-1-57685-694-9 (pbk. : alk. paper)
  ISBN-10: 1-57685-694-1 (pbk. : alk. paper)
  1. Aliens—United States—Popular works.   2. Political refugees—
Legal status, laws, etc.—United States—Popular works.   3. Green cards—
Popular works.   I. LearningExpress (Organization)
  KF4840.U478 2009
  342.7308'3—dc22

                                                          2009016511

Printed in the United States of America

9 8 7 6 5 4 3 2 1

First Edition

ISBN 978-1-57685-694-9

For information on LearningExpress, other LearningExpress products, or bulk
sales, please write to us at:
    2 Rector Street
    26th Floor
    New York, NY 10006

Or visit us at:
    www.learnatest.com

CONTENTS

INTRODUCTION

THE UNITED STATES is a nation of immigrants. Today, about one of every eight people in the U.S. population is foreign born. In 2007, 1,052,415 people became lawful permanent residents. Soon, you, too, will be a valued part of this land.

To do that, you must have permission to live and work in the United States. For newcomers who want to be here forever, that means getting a green card, a process that sometimes seems to take forever. But the result will be worth it. This book can help you on your way to becoming a legal and permanent United States resident.

How to Use This Book

For many people, getting a green card may take months or even years. It can be a complicated ordeal. Government websites offer information you need, but this information is scattered over many sections and pages—and you need a computer to access it. Using this book will make going through the green card process easier for you.

Chapter 1 briefly explains the history of immigration to the United States. Knowing how and why millions of people came here before you should help you to better understand your part in American history.

Even if you speak fluent English, you may come across unfamiliar words related to the green card process. Chapter 2 gives you a list of important words.

In Chapters 3 and 4, you'll find out exactly what a green card is, its history, who is eligible to get one, and a step-by-step description of the application process. If you're not sure you want or need to be a permanent resident, this section gives the reasons why green cards are important.

Chapter 5 takes you on the path to getting a green card through family members and explains the preference system.

Go to Chapter 6 if you plan to get your green card through marriage or as a fiancé(e).

Chapter 7 explains how your children can become permanent residents. Here, you'll also read about the new rules for adopting orphans.

Many people want green cards so they can get a job in the United States or to invest in its businesses. Chapter 8 tells you how that works.

Chapter 9 explains the immigration process for refugees and political asylees.

Chapter 10 gives information to those wanting to immigrate under the registry provision, to special immigrants, and to Iraqis and Afghans who helped the U.S. Armed Forces.

For those willing to take a chance, Chapter 11 describes the Diversity Visa Lottery.

Anyone trying to get a green card is likely to have a lot of questions. Chapter 12 lists some of the most common ones as well as easy-to-understand answers.

Any system run by the federal (national) government involves many rules that must be carefully followed. You may need a lawyer to help you get through the green card process. Chapter 13 will explain the rules and the forms you will need for this process.

And, yes, there is a light at the end of the tunnel. Just a few more steps on the path to a green card. We'll go there with you.

The end of this handy book provides addresses, phone numbers, and resources you may need. You'll also find samples of forms like those you'll be filling out, so that you can get to know them.

CHAPTER 1

A Short History of Immigration to the United States

We on this continent should never forget that men first crossed the Atlantic not to find soil for their ploughs but to secure liberty for their souls.

—Robert J. McCracken, Scottish-American minister

EVERY YEAR MORE than one million legal immigrants seek safety, freedom, prosperity, and "liberty for their souls" in the United States. Here they hope to find a real chance to better their own lives and those of their families.

Immigrants today may face tough times just as they did in centuries past. America's streets aren't paved with gold, as stories used to claim. But newcomers like you usually find a nation that is generous and friendly.

Immigrants—those who have come willingly and those who came as slaves—helped build the United States. When strength and vitality were needed to construct bridges, roads, railroads, and buildings across the growing country, workers were welcomed. For example, in the mid-1800s, Chinese workers in the West helped lay tracks for the first railroads to run from the west coast to the east coast.

Yet when that backbreaking labor ended, so did the workers' welcome. In 1882, the U.S. Congress reduced the number of Chinese who could settle here. It was the only time U.S. immigration policies were directed at one group. People who had arrived earlier seemed to forget why they themselves had come to this young nation and why they remained here. Irish Catholics were also the target of strong feelings against immigrants in the mid-1800s. "No Irish need apply," said job signs in some northeastern cities. Immigrants may look different or have different customs. Prejudice is the result of ignorance and of fear. Now, as in the past, some Americans are afraid of what they do not recognize or understand.

Immigrants slowly arrived in the wide open spaces and growing cities even before there was a United States. Starting in the 1600s and continuing into the early 1800s, pioneers left their homes in Northern and Western Europe to help establish this country. They came from what are today Germany, France, the Netherlands, and Russia; the largest number came from England, Ireland, Wales, and Scotland.

The trickle of people became a flood. In 1820, just over 8,000 immigrants settled here. The number grew to 84,000 within 20 years and continued to grow until millions joined the migration. Earlier immigrants, who were mainly farmers, were joined in the Midwest, the breadbasket of America, by Swedes, Norwegians, Danes, and Germans. Others, from Poland, Italy, Greece, Hungary, and Slavic countries, found jobs in growing industries—creating textiles and garments, assembling cars, digging for coal, and milling steel.

The invitation to join in was taken back—in part—by the National Origins Act of 1924 (first passed in 1921). It reduced the number of people who could come here, especially from Asia (hardly any), and Eastern and Southern Europe. Until 1965, when the National Origins Act was replaced with a system more like the one we have today, there were a few exceptions to the law—for some refugees of World War II and the Holocaust; for those seeking asylum from Communism, especially in the 1950s; and for Cubans after the revolution in 1960.

After 1970, the immigration pattern changed again. The United States has since been enriched by people from the continent of Africa, and from Korea, Pakistan, the Philippines, China, and India.

Like those before them, many immigrants today have endured hardships—fleeing hateful governments, deadly fighting, unending poverty, or failing crops. But, like them, you will not give up. You will study English. You will work hard. You will learn about your new home and its customs. And, chances are, you will lead a comfortable life.

Immigrants keep arriving. One study states that the number of foreign-born people in the United States has grown by 57% since the 1990s. No longer are we are a nation made up mainly of people whose ancestors came from just one part of the world. We are the world. We are from everywhere, far more diverse than we have ever been. And that is what makes us proud to have you join us.

CHAPTER 2

Words You Need to Know

MANY OF THESE words have more than one meaning. The meanings here deal only with immigration and the process of getting a green card.

☆ **ADVANCE PAROLE:** permission from the Department of Homeland Security to return to the United States after travel abroad

The permission must be requested and received before a person leaves the United States. People who may need advance parole include those on a K-1 visa, asylum applicants, parolees, people with Temporary Protected Status (TPS), and some people trying to adjust status while they are in the United States. Without advance parole, these people may be unable to return.

☆ **AFFIDAVIT** *(affi dayvit)*: the written version of sworn statement

The sponsor of an immigrant has to provide an affidavit that he or she can afford to support that person.

☆ **AGENT**: an individual who represents the applicant if the applicant doesn't have a lawyer

The agent is the person to whom all forms and letters are sent and who pays the fees. The agent does not have to be a lawyer, but can be the applicant, the petitioner, or anyone else who is trusted and reliable.

☆ **ALIEN** *(ale yen)*: a citizen of another country, a foreign national

☆ **AMNESTY** *(am nuh stee)*: pardon or act of forgiveness by the U.S. government

Aliens who have been living here illegally—without permission— for a long time may apply for amnesty if one is being offered.

☆ **APPLICANT**: a person who applies for a visa

☆ **APPLICATION**: a written request for a document such as a green card

☆ **APPOINTMENT PACKAGE**: the letter and documents giving a visa applicant information for his or her interview

The package includes the date of the interview and tells how to prepare for it.

☆ **ASYLUM** *(a sy lum)*: a place of safety

For people facing danger in their countries, the United States may provide a place to go that provides asylum from the threat of violence.

☆ **BENEFICIARY:** the applicant for a visa who is named in a petition filed with the USCIS, the United States Citizenship and Immigration Service

☆ **BIOMETRICS:** unique biological information used to identify individuals

No one else in the world has the same information. That means it is a useful way to check identity. The best known biometric is the fingerprint, but others include facial recognition and iris (eye) scans.

☆ **BUREAUCRACY** *(bue rahk reh see)*: a system of administration with official procedures that must be followed

A government bureaucracy involves many rules, many people, and many forms and other pieces of paper, which are among the reasons getting a visa takes so long. You may also notice that one sign of a bureaucracy is its wide use of initials (acronyms). As an applicant for a permanent immigrant visa, those you should know include the following (which are explained in this chapter): USCIS, DHS, DOS, TPS, and IR.

☆ **BIA:** Board of Immigration Appeals

☆ **CASE NUMBER:** the number that the National Visa Center (NVC) gives to every immigrant petition

Each case number has three letters followed by ten numbers. The letters stand for the foreign embassy or consulate that will take care of the immigrant visa.

Example: MNL stands for the U.S. embassy in Manila.

The first four of the ten numbers tell the year the case started. The other numbers give officials more information that will help them keep track of the case.

☆ **CHILD:** Immigration rules define children in many different ways. In some cases, a child may be someone who is older than 21—actually an adult. A child is almost always considered an immediate relative. (See Chapters 5 and 7.)

☆ **DEMOCRACY:** government of, for, and by the people

☆ **DEPARTMENT OF HOMELAND SECURITY (DHS):** three groups (organizations) that take care of everything to do with immigration

These groups are the United States Citizenship and Immigration Services (USCIS), Customs and Border Protection (CBP), and Immigration and Customs Enforcement (ICE).

The DHS was formed after September 11, 2001. It is responsible for watching over the stricter immigration rules that took effect after that date. Before 2003, the USCIS was called the Immigration and Naturalization Service (INS).

☆ **DEPARTMENT OF STATE (DOS):** the U.S. government department in charge of international affairs

☆ **DEPORT:** to banish from a country

☆ **DERIVATIVE BENEFICIARIES:** dependents, such as a spouse or child, who get their status from the principal, or main, beneficiary

Example: If the principal beneficiary received refugee status, his wife and children will also receive it as derivative beneficiaries.

☆ **DOMICILE:** the place where a person has his or her main residence. The person must plan to live in that residence in the future.

Example: Before the USCIS gives a visa, the sponsor must have a domicile in the United States and must live here. In some cases, it is possible for the sponsor to have a domicile here while temporarily living overseas.

☆ **ELIGIBLE:** qualified or allowed by the rules

☆ **FISCAL YEAR:** the United States government's official, or fiscal, year starts on October 1 and ends on September 30 of the following year

☆ **FRAUD** *(frawd)*: an action that cheats or deceives.

☆ **IMMIGRANT:** person from a foreign country who has permission to live and work in the United States

☆ **INADMISSIBLE:** not allowed or acceptable by law

Not everyone is welcomed to the United States. The USCIS keeps a list of reasons why some applicants are inadmissible. If even one reason applies to you, you will be turned down for a green card and, most likely, for admission into the United States.

☆ **IR:** acronym for Immediate Relative (spouse or children)

☆ **LAWFUL PERMANENT RESIDENT (LPR):** a person who has a green card

This book mainly uses the term *permanent residents.*

☆ **LEGAL/ILLEGAL:** lawful/against the law

☆ **NONIMMIGRANT VISA:** a visa that allows most visitors to stay in the United States for a limited time

Visitors could be here on tourist visas, for example, or student visas. People who stay longer than their visa allows become illegal aliens.

Visas give visitors the chance to see if they'd like to stay in the United States at a later time and apply then for a green card. Tourists from certain nations don't need visas to enter this country. This is part of the Visa Waiver Program.

☆ **PERMANENT RESIDENT:** a person who has moved to the United States and has a green card

The U.S. government refers to such a person as a lawful, or legal, permanent resident.

☆ **PETITION** *(peh tish in)*: to appeal to authority or apply for or request something

☆ **POSTS:** American embassies, consulates, or missions in other countries

Not all these sites are posts that issue visas.

☆ **PRINCIPAL APPLICANT:** the person for whom a petition is filed

A U.S. citizen may file a petition for his or her married son to move here. The son is the principal applicant. If a business files a petition for a worker, the worker is the principal applicant.

☆ **PRIORITY DATE:** the date on which an immigrant visa petition is filed for a relative

This is also the term used for the date that an employer filed a labor certificate with the Department of Labor (DOL).

☆ **PUBLIC CHARGE:** a person who depends on the government for benefits that pay for food or housing

Fear of being called a "public charge" keeps many aliens from asking for benefits that they have the right to receive. For more information about this situation, go to www.uscis.gov. Look under services & benefits/green card. Or call 800-375-5283 (customer service).

☆ QUOTA *(kwo ta)*: the maximum (highest) number admitted

Only a certain number of immigrant visas are offered to some countries, such as China and India, which have had a high number of immigrants. Once that quota is reached, no more will be issued in a fiscal year.

☆ SPONSOR *(spon sir)*: backer

The law says that sponsors (also called petitioners) must be able to support the immigrants they want to bring to the United States. The form to file for this is **I-864**, Affidavit of Support.

☆ SPOUSE *(spowss)*: legally married husband or wife

Partners who live together do not qualify as spouses for immigration purposes. Common-law spouses may qualify as immediate relatives, depending on the laws of the country where the common-law marriage took place. Polygamous marriages are not allowed. Only the first spouse can be an immediate relative.

☆ STATUS *(stah tus)*: legal standing

The status of a visa holder is an important detail. Every person who receives a visa gets it for an exact reason or category and must follow the rules for that category. For example, people who visit this country on a tourist visa may only stay here for as long as the visa says they can. If they stay longer, they can get into trouble with immigration officials and may never be able to get a green card.

☆ **TEMPORARY PROTECTED STATUS (TPS):** granted to people fleeing from disasters or war, this status does not lead to a green card. It offers people who cannot return home for a limited amount of time a temporary place of safety.

☆ **THIRD COUNTRY NATIONAL:** someone who is not a United States citizen or a citizen of the country in which the visa application is being made.

Example: Suppose you are a Moroccan visiting Canada. If you apply for a visa to visit the United States while you are in Canada, you are considered a third country national.

☆ **USCIS:** United States Citizenship and Immigration Service, part of the Department of Homeland Security

This agency is called the CIS for short on some U.S. websites and in this book.

☆ **VERIFY** *(vahr eh fie)*: prove or swear to the truth of a statement

☆ **VISA** *(vee zah)*: the document that says a foreign person is eligible to enter the United States

Permission to go beyond an airport, port, or border crossing can only be given by immigration officers at the port of entry. These officers also let foreigners know how long their visa says they may stay.

☆ **WAIVER** *(way ver)*: the giving up of a right or claim; also, a document giving up a right or claim

The U.S. government has a visa waiver program, which allows visitors from certain countries to come here without a visa.

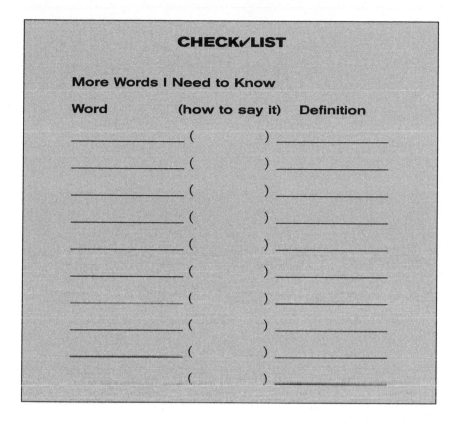

CHECK✓LIST

More Words I Need to Know

Word	(how to say it)	Definition
_____	(	) _____
_____	(	) _____
_____	(	) _____
_____	(	) _____
_____	(	) _____
_____	(	) _____
_____	(	) _____
_____	(	) _____
_____	(	) _____
	(	) _____

CHAPTER 3

What Is a Green Card?

[American citizenship] demands the best that men and women have to give. But it likewise awards its partakers the best that there is on Earth.

—Calvin Coolidge, 30th president of the United States

THE GREEN CARD has been pink, it has been blue, it has been white, and, yes, it has even been green. But no matter what its color, this little card is one of the most important documents you'll ever have if you want to be in the United States for the rest of your life.

Green card is another name for a lawful permanent resident card. It has also been called an alien registration receipt card and I-551. The first alien registration receipt cards were given out as part of the Alien Registration Act of 1940. This was about a year before the United States entered World War II, a time when there was great fear about danger from foreigners, especially people from enemy nations. The Alien Registration Act forced all immigrants, no matter where they came from, to register with the U.S. government. The Immigration and Naturalization Service (INS), which is now the USCIS, was in charge. At that time, immigrants weren't considered legal or illegal; everyone was legal and had to register. After the INS processed their registration forms, immigrants received a receipt. These receipts were the earliest versions of green cards.

In 1945, when World War II ended, many people, especially those made homeless during the war, wanted to live in the United States. A wave of immigrants flooded the United States, just as it had in times past. The INS began to issue different kinds of cards to different kinds of immigrants. These cards were the first green cards as we know them today. Every ten years or so since then, the color has changed. But it is still called a green card. Having one means you are a lawful permanent resident of the United States. You now have the privilege to live and work here under the protection of U.S. laws.

More Reasons Why It's Great to Have a Green Card

◆ You have almost all the rights of a U.S. citizen. The main exceptions: You cannot vote. You cannot run for elected office. You cannot carry a U.S. passport.

◆ You can sponsor your husband or wife and unmarried children under the age of 21 years old, so they too can become permanent residents. Even if you die or lose your job, your family will keep its green cards.

◆ You can work at any job for which you are hired. Immigration or law enforcement officials should never trouble you, your boss, or the company for which you work. To work, all you need is a temporary work permit, which is called an Employment Authorization Document (EAD).

◆ Having a green card allows you to hold jobs that need security clearance. This means that an agency like the FBI has looked into your background and has found nothing illegal (unlawful) or dangerous.

◆ You may start your own business.

◆ You may leave the United States for a certain amount of time to visit another country. When you return, you will have the same standing (being a permanent resident) that you did when you left.

◆ You may apply for financial aid from the government to help pay for your education.

◆ After living in this country for five years, you may file for U.S. citizenship.

Rights and Responsibilities

Having a green card gives you important rights. It also gives you responsibilities.

◆ You must follow all the laws of this country and the city and state you live in. If you commit a crime, you could be deported.

◆ The United States must be your main residence even if you leave for up to two years. That means you must have a home here (a house or apartment, for example), a job, or a family— a permanent tie to the United States.

◆ If you move, you must report your change of address to the USCIS.

◆ During the time you are applying for a green card (the time your visa is pending), you need special permission to leave this country. You can file **Form I-131**, which is a reentry permit that allows you to return.

◆ It is important to keep your green card up-to-date by renewing it in time—in some cases every two years or every ten years. You need to start doing this three months before the due date. So you must give yourself time to prepare any documents or other paperwork.

◆ You need a Social Security number and card to pay taxes and usually to get a job. To find out more, go to www.social security.gov or call 800-772-1213. Then, if you've worked for at least ten years before you retire, you'll have earned Social Security benefits.

◆ You must pay city, state, and U.S. taxes on all your yearly (annual) income no matter where you earned it. The Internal Revenue Service is in charge of taxation. You can find more information (and the correct forms to file) at www.irs.gov or call 800-829-1040.

◆ This country no longer drafts men into the army. Joining is voluntary. But men between the ages of 18 and 26, including those who have green cards, must sign up with the Selective Service. The website for the Selective Service is www.sss.gov or call 847-688-6888.

◆ Do you want to work as a real estate agent or insurance agent, or other professional? The state you live in may require that you have a green card before it gives you a license.

◆ Insurance companies may ask to see your green card before you can buy health, life, or car insurance.

What May Stop You from Getting or Keeping a Green Card?

You will get into big trouble, such as being deported, if you do any of the following:

◆ lie to officials to get immigration benefits for yourself or for a friend or relative

◆ spend most of your time drunk or using illegal drugs

◆ marry more than one person at a time

◆ stop paying child or spousal support

◆ assault a relative

◆ don't pay taxes or file federal, state, or city returns

◆ smuggle someone into the United States (even if the person is related to you and even if you are not paid to do it)

What a Green Card Looks Like

The look of the green card changes as technology changes. The current card can be read by machines. On it are the immigrant's photo, fingerprints, and signature. If you look at it closely, you'll see little patterns. They help make the card difficult to copy.

What about Photos?

The USCIS has strict rules about the photographs you submit. For more information, go to http://travel.state.gov/visa/guide/guide_3888.html. This is a Department of State page that deals with Visa Photo Guide Frequently Asked Questions. Not all the questions will apply to you, but much of the information will be helpful. If you can't get to a computer before you have your photo taken, use a shop or department that takes passport photos. The people there should know what to do.

Do

➤ have your photos taken by a real photographer who knows about taking passport-type photos

➤ Make sure the photographer knows all the USCIS rules for acceptable poses, acceptable clothing, photo size and dimensions, lighting, clarity, and digital resolution.

➤ take a color photo with a plain white background

➤ print several copies of the exact same photo

Don't

➤ spend money on a fancy studio shot

➤ have a friend take your photo with a personal camera

➤ use a photo booth

➤ submit photos that look the same but aren't exactly alike

➤ retouch the photo.

CHAPTER 4

Getting a Green Card: General Information

EACH OF THE NEXT EIGHT CHAPTERS gives detailed steps to getting green cards for certain categories. The following pages give you the general steps that almost everyone must follow, as well as information about what happens after you take the first step.

1. If you want to be an immigrant, a sponsor such as a relative or the person for whom you'll be working, must send a visa petition for you to the USCIS. (Some applicants such as investors, priority workers, diversity immigrants, and some special immigrants can send their own petitions.)
2. The USCIS will notify the person who filed the petition for you if it has been received and then if it has been approved.
3. Approved petitions go to the National Visa Center, which is part of the Department of State.

See the USCIS website: How do I Become a Lawful Permanent Resident . . . ?

4. Your petition stays there until it is given an immigrant visa number. The number of immigrant visas issued every year is limited. So, most immigrants are placed on long waiting lists. Among those who don't have to wait for a number are immediate relatives of U.S. citizens.

5. In the meantime, approved visa petitions are placed in the order that they were filed. The filing date is called the priority date.

6. Check the Visa Bulletin to find out about when you might receive your visa number. (See Appendix B.)

7. If you are outside the United States, you will be told when to go to the U.S. consulate in your area to finish the process for your immigrant visa.

   If you are in the United States, it's time to apply for an adjustment to permanent resident status.

8. In time, you will receive your lawful permanent resident card. Hooray for your patience and determination!

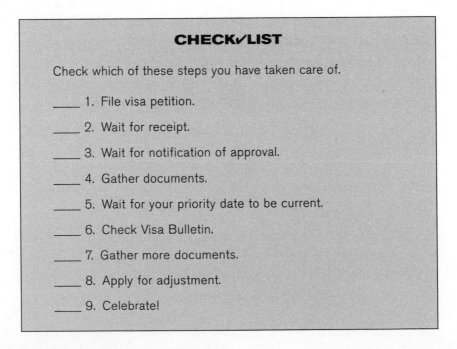

CHECK✓LIST

Check which of these steps you have taken care of.

_____ 1. File visa petition.

_____ 2. Wait for receipt.

_____ 3. Wait for notification of approval.

_____ 4. Gather documents.

_____ 5. Wait for your priority date to be current.

_____ 6. Check Visa Bulletin.

_____ 7. Gather more documents.

_____ 8. Apply for adjustment.

_____ 9. Celebrate!

If You Change Your Address

If you have a case pending, you must let the USCIS know within ten days of moving that you have changed your address. To do that, you must follow two steps.

1. You must file Form **AR-11**, Alien's Change of Address Card. You can do this online to change your address on the USCIS master list at https://egov.uscis.gov/crisgwi/go?action=coa .Terms.

2. You must also call the customer service center at 800-375-5283 to change the address on your application.

If you are not a U.S. citizen, you will need:

➤ your receipt notice or other notice you received from the USCIS that shows your receipt number*

➤ your new address

➤ your old address

➤ names and biographical information of family members for whom you filed a petition

➤ date when you last entered the United States

➤ port of entry (land, sea, or air) where you last entered the United States

A refugee or asylee must send a letter to the local immigration office to inform them about his or her new home. On the outside of

---

*If you cannot find a receipt number, here's what to do: If you paid by check, look at the back of the canceled check that was returned to you by your bank. On the back is the 13-digit USCIS receipt number. It looks like this (with different numbers, of course): ABC 01 23456789. If you paid by money order, call USCIS customer service at 800-375-5283. The person answering the phone will enter your new address for you.

(continues)

the envelope, write Attention: Change of Address. In your letter, include the following information:

➤ your name as it is on your I-94
➤ your A (Alien) number
➤ your old and new addresses
➤ the date on which you will live in your new home

Stay Up-to-Date

Check the USCIS website (under Immigration Forms) often or call 800-375-5283 to make sure the forms and fees haven't changed. If you don't have a computer and can't get to one, and you can't get through to customer service, ask someone you trust to go online and check for you. It is very important to have up-to-date information. Sending the wrong form or paying the wrong fee could make a long process even longer.

CHAPTER 5

Paths to a Green Card: Family Ties

You cannot spill a drop of American blood without spilling the blood of the whole world. . . . We are not a nation, so much as a world.

—Herman Melville, American writer

THE UNITED STATES offers immigrants several ways to get green cards. The paths to a green card are explained in this and the following seven chapters.

Here is information that you must know if you are trying to bring a member of your family to the United States or if you want to become an immigrant yourself.

The relative who is your sponsor must file an **I-130**, Petition for Alien Relative, for you. It must be sent, with proof of your relationship to the sponsor, to the USCIS.

Example: Suppose your mother is your sponsor. You can show a copy of your birth certificate to prove how you are related. For other kinds of proof, see the list on page 42.

See the USCIS website: Immigration Through a Family Member OR, Department of State website: Immigrant Visa for a Spouse (IR1 or CR1)

Which relatives are eligible to sponsor you? (Or, if you are an immigrant, which relatives can you sponsor?)

A sponsor must be a citizen or have a green card. Whom someone is allowed to sponsor depends on whether the sponsor is a citizen or has a green card (permanent resident).

Example 1: If the sponsor is a U.S. citizen, he or she can petition for a wife or husband or a fiancé(e) to be an immigrant. U.S. citizens can also petition for: unmarried or married children, the brother or sister of an adult sponsor, the parent of adult sponsor.

Example 2: If the sponsor is a permanent resident, she or he may petition for a spouse and unmarried children.

Example 3: If you were married to a U.S. citizen who died after you lived together for at least two years, you can file a petition for yourself. The filing has to be done within two years of your spouse's death. So, if your husband or wife died on May 3, 2008, your petition must be filed by May 3, 2010.

A sponsor must prove a close connection to the person being sponsored. The sponsor must fill out **Form I-864** or **I-864-EZ**, Affidavit of Support, proving that he or she is able to support the relative at 125% above the official poverty level. "The poverty level is the lowest income acceptable for a family of a certain size so that the family does not live in poverty," according to guidelines of the U.S. Department of Health and Human Services. The department publishes an annual list that defines poverty levels. When you go to a consulate, an officer there uses those numbers to decide whether or not your sponsor earns enough money to support you, the new immigrant.

If you look at the tables that follow in this chapter, you'll see the numbers used in 2009. (Notice that the numbers are higher for Hawaii and Alaska.)

Example 1: Suppose three people (including you) are living in the sponsor's household. That means your sponsor would have to earn $22,887 according to the 2009 guidelines. If you have a legal job, you can add your earnings to the total to reach the amount needed.

To reach the amount needed, the sponsor can also include assets, such as a home or a car. If assets are used, it must be possible to sell them for cash within a year. The assets have to equal five times the difference between the poverty guidelines amount and what the household actually earns (income). This is cut to three times for immediate relatives, such as husbands and wives.

$22,887   guidelines amount for a household of three people
−15,000   income of sponsor
$ 7,887   difference between two figures
$ 7,887 × 5 = $39,435
The assets have to be worth at least $39,435.

Someone who meets the requirement for 125% income may be a cosponsor or joint sponsor. If one cosponsor does not meet the income minimum, a second cosponsor may be added. The cosponsor(s) must also fill out an Affidavit of Support.

Others living in the household, 18 years and older, may add their incomes so that the 125% figure is met. They must file **Form I-864A**, Contract Between Sponsor and Household Member.

The EZ form is shorter and easier to fill out than I-864. To use the EZ version, the sponsor may only petition for one person and must earn enough money to support the applicant without help from anyone else.

A small group of people is exempt (excused) from filling out I-864. They must file **Form I-864W** instead. These people include:

◆ immigrants who qualify for U.S. citizenship right after they become permanent residents

◆ immigrants who have worked in the United States for about ten years (long enough to qualify for Social Security)
◆ widows or widowers of U.S. citizens who submit petitions for themselves
◆ abused spouses or children

2009 Poverty Guidelines for the 48 contiguous states, the District of Columbia, Puerto Rico, U.S. Virgin Islands, and Guam

Persons in family	100% of Poverty Line*	125% of Income
2	14,570	18,212
3	18,310	22,887
4	22,050	27,562
5	25,790	32,237
6	29,530	36,912
7	33,270	41,587
8	37,010	46,262

For families with more than 8 people, add $3,740 for each additional person.

*For sponsors on active duty in the U.S. armed forces who are petitioning for their spouse or child

2009 Poverty Guidelines for Alaska

Persons in family	100% of Poverty Line*	125% of Income
2	18,210	22,763
3	22,890	28,613
4	27,570	34,463
5	32,250	40,313
6	36,930	46,163

| 7 | 41,610 | 52,013 |
| 8 | 46,290 | 57,863 |

For families with more than 8 people, add $4,680 for each additional person ($5,850 at 125%).

*For sponsors on active duty in the U.S. armed forces who are petitioning for their spouse or child.

2008 Poverty Guidelines for Hawaii

Persons in family	100% of Poverty Line*	125% of Income
2	16,760	20,950
3	21,060	26,325
4	25,360	31,700
5	29,960	37,075
6	33,960	42,450
7	38,260	47,825
8	42,560	53,200

For families with more than 8 people, add $4,300 for each additional person ($5,375 at 125%).

*For sponsors on active duty in the U.S. armed forces who are petitioning for their spouse or child.

Source: Federal Register, Vol. 73, No. 15, January 23, 2008, pp. 3971–3972, U.S. Department of State

In many cases (but not all), U.S. immigration officials try to keep families together. An **immediate relative** (IR) is the closest relative—the husband or wife, widow or widower, or unmarried child under 21 years old—of a U.S. citizen. If the U.S. citizen is 21 or older, his or her parents are the immediate relatives. Immediate relatives don't have to wait for an immigrant visa number to become available. They are placed at the top of the immigration preference list, which means they get first preference and the best chance to quickly receive an immigrant visa number if they need one.

How to Prove a Family Tie

As with every other part of the immigration process, it's very important to submit the correct documents. If you are trying to get your green card by using a family relationship, you must have official documents that show you are related. Here is what you need, depending on who is sponsoring you:

➤ your original birth certificate

Don't send the original. Send a copy. Keep the original in a safe place that you can get to in case you have to take it with you to a USCIS interview.

➤ a marriage certificate or the death certificate (for your deceased spouse)

This must be an official document from your country. It must be marked with a seal that shows your country's government issued it. The USCIS may not accept a certificate without a seal.

What if you can't find the original documents? Don't panic. Request duplicates (copies) from your government if possible. (The copies must have the right seals on them.) If it isn't possible to get copies, you can provide the next best evidence (secondary evidence)—documents that are not official, but are still trustworthy. These could include:

notes in a family Bible
school records
government census records
religious records, such as baptismal or circumcision certificate
notarized sworn statements from two witnesses to the event (birth, death, marriage) you are trying to prove took place

If you still need documents, you may find help at the Department of State website. Go to http://travel.state.gov/visa/frvi/reciprocity_3272.html. It will, in most cases, help you find the documents you thought might be lost forever.

Every year, green card holders' spouses and unmarried children under 21 are eligible for 88,000 immigrant visas. Unmarried children over 21 years old qualify for 26,000 visas a year. In 2002, when the Child Status Protection Act was passed, the sons and daughters of American citizens or permanent residents got good news. Citizens' children who turn 21 while they're waiting for their visas to come through, can now keep their immediate relative status. Before 2002, turning 21 meant a young adult would have to drop to a lower preference category. (You will learn more about preference categories in the following pages.)

The situation is a little more complicated for the children of green card holders (permanent residents). Children who celebrate their twenty-first birthday after their priority date becomes current, but who don't yet have their green cards, have a year to file for them.

Some family members may be close—but, to the USCIS, they aren't close enough to be considered immediate relatives. So they don't qualify for green cards given to people with family ties.

Example 1: The grandparents, aunts, uncles, cousins, nieces, and nephews of U.S. citizens are not immediate relatives.

Example 2: The parents, brothers, sisters, or fiancé(e) of a person with a green card are not immediate relatives.

Based on the preferences listed below, the Department of State will decide if an immigrant visa number is available for you right away. When a number is available, you can apply to have it assigned to you. The best way to find out what's happening to your number is to check the Visa Bulletin. (See Appendix B for more about the Visa Bulletin.)

Where's My Number?

To find out what is happening with a visa number, check the Visa Bulletin of the Department of State.

When a visa number becomes available to you, there are two ways to claim it:

◆ If you are in the United States on a nonimmigrant visa, apply to change your status. You will then become a lawful permanent resident. This is called adjustment of status.

◆ If you are outside the United States, go to the U.S. consulate for the area you live in so that you can complete the visa process. This is called consular processing.

The USCIS uses the preference system to decide the order in which relatives are eligible for immigration. "Preference" means "favorite" or "first choice." The immigration system uses first, second, third, and fourth as the order in which certain people are chosen. No matter what your preference category, you still need a petition filed for you. And the sponsor has to prove the relationship. But, depending on which category you are in, you may not have to wait for a visa number to become available.

Family First Preference (F1) is for parents, unmarried children of U.S. citizens (IR), and their children.

Number of visas available for this category: about 23,400
Waiting time: about five years
Waiting time exceptions: Mexicans, 14 years; Filipinos, 15 years

Family Second Preference (F2) is for the husbands or wives and unmarried children (2A) or unmarried adult children (2B) of lawful permanent residents.

Number of visas available for this category: about 114,200
Waiting time: about five years for unmarried children under 21 years old; about ten years for unmarried children over 21 years old
Waiting time exceptions: Mexicans, seven years for children under 21 years old and spouses, 15 years for adult unmarried children

Family Third Preference (F3) is for married children of U.S. citizens and their spouses and children.

> Number of visas available for this category: about 23,400
> Waiting time: about eight years
> Waiting time exceptions: Mexicans, 13 years; 18 years for Filipinos

Family Fourth Preference (F4) is for brothers and sisters of U.S. citizens and their spouses and children. The U.S. citizen must be 21 years old or older before he or she can submit a petition.

> Number of visas available for this category: about 65,000
> Waiting time: from 10 to 24 years

Preferences can change. Here are three examples of how this can happen. As you can see, marriage and divorce have a great effect on how long it may take to get a green card.

> *Example 1: The divorce of the son or daughter of a U.S. citizen changes the child's preference either to immediate relative status or to first preference.*

> *Example 2: If a U.S. citizen's adult son or daughter (older than 21), marries, the bridegroom or bride moves down to third preference.*

> *Example 3: If a U.S. citizen's child who is under 21 marries, he or she moves down to third preference.*

The Petition Process

1. **Form I-130,** the visa petition, is filed with the USCIS.
2. The USCIS approves or turns down (denies) the petition.
3. The USCIS tells the petition sponsor if the petition was approved.

4. The approved petition goes to the National Visa Center, where it waits until an immigrant visa number is available.

5. The Center tells you (the applicant) when it receives the petition and lets you know when a number is available. (These two events may be many months or years apart.)

Taking Back a Visa Petition

A visa petition can be canceled or withdrawn. This may happen if a fact in an applicant's life changes.

Example 1: The sponsor changes his mind. He must tell the USCIS that he is no longer willing to sponsor the applicant.

Example 2: If a married couple who applied under the marriage category divorces before the immigrant partner's green card is approved.

Example 3: If the sponsor who is a citizen dies before a married child receives a green card. Although another financial sponsor will have to be found, the USCIS may still allow the application to go ahead for "humanitarian reasons."

CHAPTER 6

Paths to a Green Card: Marriage

IF YOU ARE A FOREIGNER planning to marry a U.S. citizen or a permanent resident, you are in good company. Many thousands of people do that every year. As with other paths to a green card, this one involves many forms and documents—perhaps more than any other.

Your sponsor must be at least 18 years old, live in the United States, and be able to sign **Form-864**, Affidavit of Support, in order to file an immigrant visa for spouses and other relatives.

To get a green card through marriage, you must be in a legal marriage. It doesn't matter where your ceremony was performed as long as it followed the laws of your state or country. And it has to be a true marriage—getting married just to get a green card can lead to many problems.

*Example 1: **If you live abroad and are married to a U.S. citizen**, you are now an immediate relative. As soon as you file your petition,*

See the USCIS website: How Do I Bring My Fiancé(e) to the United States?

it is approved, and when you have been through the application process, you will receive your green card.

It may be possible to shorten the process time by using **Form 129-F**, the fiancé(e) visa, even if you are already married. The minute you receive a receipt notice for Form I-130 from the USCIS, file the special version of Form 129-F with the agency. Then you will have to go through consular processing. When the consulate approves your fiancé(e) visa, you may enter the United States. Once there, you can apply for your green card. When you are in the United States, you can fill out and file an adjustment of status application with the USCIS.

> *Example 2:* **If you live in the United States and are married to a U.S. citizen,** *mail your visa petition and adjustment of status package to the USCIS. It will let you know when to go to your district office for your fingerprinting appointment and for your interview. (Both spouses must attend the interview.)*

> *Example 3:* **If you live abroad and are married to a U.S. lawful permanent resident** *and your spouse filed a visa petition for you, you will be in family preference category 2A. You will have to wait until your priority date is current to apply for your green card. You will have to wait abroad, which means it may be several years before you can apply for your visa, receive your green card, and live here permanently.*

To become a permanent resident, you must enter the United States within six months after you receive your visa. If you have been married less than two years, you will become a conditional resident.

> *Example 4:* **If you are in the United States and are married to a U.S. lawful permanent resident,** *your spouse should send your petition to the USCIS. It will stay there until your priority date is current. The next step is to file a green card application—in other words, you will have to adjust status. You can do this if you have*

been living in the United States legally while your petition was being processed. (See Chapter 14 on adjusting status and consular processing.) This may be one of those times that you should talk to a lawyer. (See Chapter 13.)

Some applicants living overseas choose to use consular processing. This simply means that, after the USCIS approves your visa petition, your documents go through the U.S. consulate in your homeland instead of to a USCIS office.

The sections, "Forms and Documents You May Need" and "What Steps to Follow," later in this chapter, explain almost all you have to know about filing for a marriage-based green card. But there are, of course, exceptions.

Example 1: If your husband or wife filed a petition for you when he or she was a permanent resident, but is now a U.S. citizen, your preference category changes. Your spouse must change your petition from family second preference (F2) to immediate relative (IR). This is a good thing. You will be admitted faster. Your spouse must send proof of his or her citizenship to the National Visa Center (NVC). The proof could be a copy of the identification page of his or her passport or a copy of the naturalization certificate.

Your children are also affected by the change in status from F2 to IR. Children are included in F2 petitions. They aren't included in parents' IR petitions. If your spouse did not file separate petitions for your children when he or she was a permanent resident, that must now be done. Your spouse, who is now a citizen, must file visa petitions for each of your children (one petition for each child).

Example 2: In the case of a couple who have been married for less than two years, the spouse who arrives here on an immigrant visa is a conditional resident (CR), not an immediate relative (IR). If you have been married less than two years, you are a conditional permanent resident and your green card expires after two years. (Yes!

You are both conditional and permanent.) To become permanent, here's what you need to do. It is called removal of conditions. File **Form I-751,** *Petition to Remove the Conditions on Residence. You must do this three months (90 days) before the second anniversary of the day you received your conditional permanent residence. (Children who immigrated with you also have to petition for removal of conditions.)*

Send your documents by certified return receipt requested mail to your nearest USCIS Regional Service Center. Here is what you need to send:

◆ Form I-751, Petition to Remove the Conditions on Residence. Both you and your spouse must sign it.
◆ the fee to the USCIS
◆ proof that yours is a real marriage. To do this, you can submit all or some of the following documents from the time of your marriage:
  ➤ proof that both spouses own property together
  ➤ bills addressed to Mr. and Mrs.
  ➤ proof of joint bank accounts
  ➤ insurance policies showing both names
  ➤ birth certificate showing both parents' names
  ➤ letter from current employers on company paper giving job title, salary, and emergency contact
  ➤ will showing one spouse as beneficiary of the other

Proving Documents Are Real

On the back (never the front) of every copy that you plan to submit, carefully write or type this statement, then sign and date it: *This is an exact copy of the unchanged original document. I have the original and will submit it to immigration or consular officials on request.*

Forms and Documents You May Need for Immigration by Marriage

Forms and Documents	Who Must Provide Document
I-130, Petition for Alien Relative	sponsor
Form I-751, to remove conditions	couples married less than 2 years
G-325A, Biographic Information	applicant and spouse
I-864, Affidavit of Support	sponsor
DS-230, Parts I and **II**	applicant
valid passport	applicant
birth certificate	applicant
police certificates (applicant's police record in native country)	applicant
medical exam, vaccination report	applicant
2 passport-style photos	applicant and spouse
proof of citizenship *or* proof of permanent residency	sponsor
marriage certificate	applicant and spouse
wedding photos and so on	applicant and spouse
divorce decree from previous marriage *or* death certificate of deceased spouse	applicant
Fees	applicant and spouse

What Steps to Follow

◆ If you live in the United States, your spouse (your husband or wife) files **Form I-130.** It should be mailed to the USCIS field office that serves the area in which your spouse lives. (See Appendix B for a list of offices.)

◆ A U.S. citizen who lives in another country is sometimes allowed to file Form I-130 at a U.S. embassy or post abroad. To find post locations and to learn who is eligible to do this, go to http://travel.state.gov/travel/tips/registration_1186.html.

Warning about Fake Websites

Official government sites always end in .gov.
They never end in .com, .net, or .org. Be careful of websites that look like, but aren't, real U.S. government sites. Deal only with official U.S. government sites. Printing forms off a USCIS or Department of State site is free. Just go to www.uscis.gov to or call 800-375-5283 to get forms that are the latest versions (that's important) and free of charge.

◆ Once the local USCIS office approves the petition, the USCIS sends it to the National Visa Center (NVC).

◆ You (the applicant) must wait until your qualifying date comes up. (The qualifying date is when the NVC is ready to send the instruction package to the applicant.) The NVC will then contact you and the petitioner. You will receive your instruction package, which will give you information on how and where to pay the processing fees. **It is very important to read the instructions and carefully follow them.**

◆ After the processing fees are paid, the NVC will ask you and the petitioner for visa documentation.

◆ Documents in a foreign language must be translated into English. The translator must sign a statement that the translation is accurate and that the translator is competent (expert). The statement can be typed out as a paragraph or could look like this certificate from the Board of Immigration Appeals.

CERTIFICATE OF TRANSLATION

I, _____, am competent to translate from _____ into English, and certify that the translation is true and accurate to the best of my abilities.

_____ (signature of translator)
_____ (typed or printed name of translator)

◆ An interview is the final step in this process (as you will see below). At that time, your fingerprints will be taken (digitally, so no ink is used). The length of the interview depends on your situation. Although you have already sent many forms and documents to the USCIS, the official conducting the interview may ask for more information and you may have to supply more documents.

What to Take to Your Interview

Take clear copies with you, so the originals can be returned. Remember to ask for their return when your interview is over. (You may be given a form to fill out.) You have to submit these documents (and perhaps others) to the Department of State even if you already gave them to the CIS.

◆ Passport good for travel to the United States that is good for at least six months longer than you plan to stay. People from certain countries don't need this. See http://travel.state.gov/visa/immigrants/info/info_1339.html
◆ birth certificate
◆ divorce decree or death certificate from previous spouse. Previous marriages must have been legally ended.
◆ marriage certificate
◆ military records if you served in another nation's armed forces
◆ police certificates from each place you've lived since age 16. These certificates must state if you had a criminal record. There is much more information about this at http://travel.state.gov/visa/immigrants/info/info_1339.html. Go to National Visa Center, then FAQs.
◆ medical examination (based on instructions from the NVC) and vaccination records
◆ completed **Form I-864**, Affidavit of Support, from sponsor
◆ completed **Form DS-230, parts I and II**, Application for Immigrant Visa and Alien Registration
◆ two immigrant visa photos (signed on the back in pencil)

◆ proof of marriage and husband-wife relationship that may include
> marriage certificate
> income tax returns that are signed, dated, and approved by the Internal Revenue Service for the years of your marriage
> your wedding photos
> apartment leases or contracts signed by both spouses, along with rent or maintenance checks
> check or money order to pay immigrant processing fees

If you have a lawyer (also called an attorney), here is what will happen next:

◆ The NVC will assign a case number to your petition.
◆ The NVC will send the Affidavit of Support processing fee bill and the immigrant visa fee bill to your lawyer.
◆ After the Affidavit of Support fee is paid, the NVC will send your lawyer instructions about what to do next. **It is very important to read the instructions and carefully follow them.**
◆ Your documents will now be sent to the NVC. It will look them over and make sure that the information in them is correct and complete.
◆ When the papers are complete, the NVC will send your petition to the embassy or consulate in your country, where you will apply for a visa. For some embassies or consulates, the NVC will schedule your interview.
◆ About one month before your scheduled interview appointment with a consular officer, you, the applicant, and your lawyer will each receive an appointment letter. It will tell the date and time of your visa interview as well as instructions for getting a medical examination. (Only you, the applicant, attend the interview and exam.)

When You Need a Notary Public

A notary public isn't a lawyer as he or she is in some other countries. But if you live in the United States, you may have to find a notary public before you submit some of your documents. A notary public is a person with a license that allows him or her to confirm that an affidavit is legal or that signatures are real. Notary publics may be found in some drugstores and stationery stores or in banks. Sometimes a sign on the door will tell you one is inside. Some, but not all, notaries charge a fee for placing an official seal on your document. If you live outside the United States, a consular or embassy official may notarize your documents.

If you do not have a lawyer, here are the next steps:

◆ The NVC will assign a case number to your petition.
◆ The NVC will send **Form DS-3032**, Choice of Address and Agent, to you (the applicant) and the Affidavit of Support processing fee bill to the petitioner.
◆ The NVC will send the immigrant visa processing fee bill to the agent you chose. (The agent does not have to be a lawyer.) See Appendix C for step-by-step instructions on how to pay your fees.
◆ After you pay the visa application fee, the NVC will send instructions to your agent that will explain how to file your documents. **It is very important to read the instructions and carefully follow them.**
◆ The documents will be filed with the NVC, which will look them over to make sure that their information is correct and complete.
◆ After the Affidavit of Support processing fee is paid, the NVC will send you a letter explaining what happens next.
◆ When the papers are complete, the NVC will send your petition to the embassy or consulate where you will apply for a visa. For some embassies or consulates, the NVC will schedule your interview.

◆ About one month before your scheduled interview appointment with a consular officer, you, the applicant, and your agent will each receive an appointment letter. It will give you the date and time of your visa interview as well as instructions for getting a medical examination.

☆ ☆ ☆

YOU HAVE TO REALLY WANT THIS

I'VE HEARD THAT it's much harder now to get a green card. But, when I got mine in the mid-1990s, it was plenty hard. First of all, I was living in Guyana then and it took me more than a day to get to the U.S. embassy and back each time I went. I had to take two ferries and four buses. That was okay when the weather was good, but when it rained, forget it! My wife, who was an American citizen, and I were married in the United States by a famous priest from Guyana. When I went for my marriage interview, I brought all kinds of documents with me. But that wasn't enough. In the end, the priest came with me and told them that I had definitely married for love. Which I did.

—Rudolf, from Guyana

☆ ☆ ☆

If You Use a Fiancé(e) Visa

Some couples who want to marry and live in the United States choose to file a fiancé(e) visa, **Form I-129F**, Petition for Alien Fiancé(e). The fiancé(e) visa was first used a few years ago in an effort by the government to make the immigration process go faster. It is not clear, though, if it really works that way. It may be just as slow and maybe even more costly. (It means filing extra paperwork.)

You may use the fiancé(e) visa only once. If you leave the United States before you are married, you may have to get a new visa in order to return. The citizen to whom you are engaged must apply for **Form**

I-130. After that is filed and received, **Form I-129F** must be filed if you, the fiancé(e), are not a citizen but want to be married in the United States. Once the petitions are approved, you must get a visa from the U.S. embassy or consulate in your country.

You must be unmarried and able to prove that if you had a previous marriage, it was annulled or ended in divorce or the death of a spouse. Before filing for the visa, you and your fiancé(e) must have met in person within two years of filing for the visa. There are exceptions, of course.

Example: The two-year time period can be waived if spending time with your fiancé(e) goes against your customs or if it would have been a terrible hardship to meet. Still, if you look at the form, you will see that you must explain how you met and other details about your relationship.

Until you get married, you are a nonimmigrant. You must be married within 90 days of your entering the United States. The 90-day limit can't be extended, so if you don't marry in time or the wedding is canceled, you must leave this country.

If you want to live and work as a permanent resident in the United States, you must apply for your green card right after your marriage. If you don't plan to do this, you will have to leave the United States. If you go ahead and apply, you will become a conditional permanent resident. (This is because you've been married less than two years.) You may also apply to bring in your unmarried children under 21 years old.

When to Contact the National Visa Center

The best answer is "never." But there are exceptions. You will have to give new information if:

➤ your address changes
➤ your life changes (you reach the age of 21, get married or divorced, or your spouse dies)

Immigration experts suggest that, soon after arriving in the United States, you should write to the local center that processed Form I-130. Inform the office that you are in the country and will be adjusting your status.

Getting a Social Security Card

Your husband or wife in the United States can help you prepare for life there by showing you how to apply for your Social Security card. You may apply for one when you file your visa Application. To find out if you need a Social Security number:

➤ Call 800-772-1213 between 7 A.M. and 7 P.M. Information is given in English and Spanish. Free interpreter services are available.

➤ Look for the address in the blue pages of your local phone book.

➤ Go to the Social Security Administration website at http://www.socialsecurity.gov or, for Spanish, go to http://www.segurosocial.gov/espanol/.

CHAPTER 7

Paths to a Green Card: Children, Orphan Immigrants

IF YOU ARE IMMIGRATING through marriage, you may bring your children with you. It doesn't matter if they are from a previous marriage or relationship, but the children must be under 21 and unmarried.

If you are marrying a U.S. citizen, your children will be considered immediate relatives of your spouse. A separate **Form I-130**, a visa petition, has to be filed for each child who is claiming to be an immediate relative. These petitions should, if possible, go in the same package as yours. If you are using a fiancé(e) visa, your spouse will also have to file separate **Form I-129F** petitions for each child, just as was done for you.

If you are marrying a permanent resident, your children are considered "derivative beneficiaries." This means that they get their status, their visa, through you, another applicant. The children won't need separate petitions or even need to prove their relationship to you. Your spouse just has to fill in the parts of Form I-130 that ask for the children's names.

The children will get the same priority date as you and will most likely get their visas at the same time, too. But what if they marry or turn 21 before that happens?

Example 1: Children under the age of 21 who marry before getting their visa can no longer be beneficiaries.

Example 2: Children who turn 21 before their priority date becomes current, change to the 2B category and cannot immigrate at the same time as you.

Once the children's visa petitions are approved, you must submit a separate application for each child—either to a U.S. consulate or to a USCIS office. If your children are too young to sign their names, you can do it for them. Just make a note that you did it.

How to Prove a Child Is Your Child

1. If the child is the unmarried son or daughter under the age of 21 of married parents: A birth certificate showing the name of the mother and child is needed if the mother files the immigration petition.

    If the father files, he must present the child's birth certificate with his name on it as well as a marriage certificate that shows the parents were married before the child was born.

2. If the parents were not married to each other when the child was born, the birth certificate is all that's needed if the mother is filing. If the mother changed her name after the child's birth, she has to show an official name-change document like a marriage certificate.

    If the father is filing and his name is on the birth certificate, that's fine. If not, it gets more complicated. He may need to have his name placed on the birth certificate to show he is the child's biological (natural) father or he may need to take a DNA test for proof. The father also has to show, with photographs or child support checks, for example, that before the child turned 18, they had a father and child relationship.

3. A child born out of wedlock (to parents who were not married to each other at the time) can be listed as a child for immigration purposes if the natural father goes through a legal process called "legitimation." The child must be under 21 and in the legal custody of the father when the process takes place. The father needs the birth certificate and the marriage certificate to prove his relationship.

4. If the child is a stepchild, the marriage between the parent and the American citizen or green card holder must have taken place before the child turned 18.

5. An adopted child must have been fully adopted before the child turned 16. The adopting parent must have lived with and had legal custody of the child for at least two years. An adopted child may have living biological parents.

6. An orphan may be considered your child if he or she has been adopted abroad by an American citizen or if the parent who is an American citizen has filed an immediate relative visa petition for the child. Then the orphan child can go to the United States for adoption by the American citizen.

7. Adopted orphans who apply for green cards face some complications. The sponsor must have had legal custody for at least two years and the adopted child must have lived with the adoptive parents in the child's country for at least two years before the petition was filed. However, permanent residents can't leave the country for two years. This is a case when you most likely need the advice of an immigration lawyer.

The Petition Process

If you are filing for your child . . .

1. Prepare **Form I-130**, Petition for Alien Relative, which will be filed with the USCIS.

2. Gather the documents that must be included in the package with Form I-130. For children who are immigrating, these documents are:
> child's birth certificate
> parents' marriage certificate
> documents that prove at least one parent's citizenship or green card
> **Form G-325A**, which includes biographic information about the child, and must be signed by him or her

For adopted children, the following documents must be included:
> adoption decree for the child before he or she was 16 years old
> proof of legal custody for at least two years
> birth certificate for the child
> proof that the adopted child has lived with the adoptive parent(s) for at least two years
> proof of the marital status of the parent who is filing the petition
> cover letter that introduces you and the child and lists all the documents included in the package.

If the unmarried child of U.S. citizens lawfully lives in the United States, is a minor, and an immediate relative, include **Form I-485,** Adjustment of Status, along with the visa petition. Follow the instruction on the form on how to mail the documents.

If the unmarried child of U.S. citizens lives abroad, the visa petition should be mailed to the USCIS Chicago lockbox.
> The USCIS will forward the petition to the parents' local field office.
> When the petition is approved, the U.S. consulate in the country where the child lives will be in charge.
> The child can then apply for an immigrant visa and green card through the consulate.

If the child's parents are green card holders and the child is married or older than 21 and an immediate relative, and lives in another country, mail the petition to the USCIS Chicago lockbox.

➤ The USCIS will forward the petition to the parents' local field office.

➤ After the petition is approved, the child's priority number will decide where he or she will be on the waiting list. When the number becomes current, the U.S. consulate in the child's native country will do the processing toward a green card.

Orphan Immigrants

In 2008, people in the United States adopted 17,438 orphan immigrants. More than 200,000 children adopted from overseas are now living in the United States. If you are seeking an orphan to join this nationwide community, here is information you should know.

A child is considered an orphan if he or she has no parents because of death, disappearance, desertion, or abandonment. An orphan may also have a single parent or unwed mother who cannot care for the child.

Permanent residents aren't allowed to file a petition for an orphan child. If a married couple is adopting, one has to be a U.S. citizen. Single parents must be at least 25 years old before filing a petition. The orphan child must be under 16, or under 18 if being adopted with a sibling.

Americans who want to adopt a child from overseas have two different intercountry adoption plans to choose from—the established orphan process and the new Hague Convention. The USCIS suggests that those interested in adopting should first decide on a specific country from which to adopt. The conventional orphan process now applies only to nations that didn't ratify the Hague Convention.

The new law about intercountry adoptions, called the Hague Convention on the Protection of Children (HCIA), went into effect in the United States on April 1, 2008. On the website of the Adoption Network Law Center, Dr. William L. Pierce wrote in 2000 that the treaty is "designed to reduce the incidence of trafficking in children and to expedite legal adoption of children across national borders. The Convention was the result of work by several dozen nations at The Hague, the capital of the Netherlands, meeting under the auspices of the Hague Conference on Private International Law (HCPIL)." The treaty affects immigrating adoptive children in the 75 countries that signed it. (See the list in the table on pages 53–54.)

As a first step in the United States, prospective adoptive parents will have to undergo background and criminal checks and a thorough home study. This process will take about three months. Once eligibility and suitability to adopt are established, procedures will be put into place, as they have been for the orphan process that has been in effect.

Following is what you should know now.

◆ The Department of State (DOS) is in charge of making the HCIA work. So, to get the latest information on it, go to http://travel.state.gov. Click on Children & Family, then on Intercountry Adoption.

◆ Adoption agencies must be accredited either by the Council on Accreditation or the Colorado Department of Human Services. This means that there are now fewer agencies. The DOS website has a list of accredited agencies.

◆ Adoption agencies must be far more timely and transparent about financial matters than they were in the past.

◆ Children about to be adopted will be more carefully screened. The HCIA wants to make sure that adoptions are in the best interests of the children. Though this will be beneficial to the children, it may cause even longer waits or great disappointment for hopeful prospective parents.

◆ Parents will know in advance whether their child is eligible to enter the United States. This will be decided by a U.S. consular officer who will issue a certificate to the child if the child has met the Convention adoption requirements.

◆ For Hague Convention adoption cases, the forms now used arc **Form I-800** and **Form I-800A**. Form I-800A, which must be filed first, determines whether prospective parents can adopt. Form I-800 is then used to determine the eligibility of the child being adopted. Two new visa categories—IH-3 and IH-4—are in effect for Convention adoptions.

◆ Some countries will be banned or have fewer children available if irregularities are proven. This could include nations that signed the Convention, but haven't followed its rules.

Countries That Signed the Hague Convention

Albania	El Salvador	Netherlands
Andorra	Estonia	New Zealand
Armenia	Finland	Norway
Australia	France	Panama
Austria	Georgia	Paraguay
Azerbaijan	Germany	Peru
Belarus	Guatemala	Philippines
Belgium	Guinea	Poland
Belize	Hungary	Portugal
Bolivia	Iceland	Romania
Brazil	India	San Marino
Bulgaria	Israel	Seychelles
Burkina Faso	Italy	Slovakia
Burundi	Kenya	Slovenia
Cambodia	Latvia	South Africa
Canada	Lithuania	Spain
Chile	Luxembourg	Sri Lanka
Colombia	Madagascar	Sweden
Costa Rica	Mali	Switzerland
Cuba	Malta	Thailand
Cyprus	Mauritius	Turkey
Czech Republic	Mexico	United Kingdom
Denmark	Moldova	United States
Dominican Republic	Monaco	Uruguay
Ecuador	Mongolia	Venezuela

What Are Transition Cases?

If an adoption case started before April 1, 2008 and the prospective parents filed the forms being used at that time (Forms I-600A and I-600), it is called a transition case. Convention processes may not apply. If I-600A was approved, it can be extended to provide more time in which the case can be completed. Parents with transition cases can receive up to two extensions and will continue to be processed as they would have been before the Convention rules went into effect.

Prospective parents who want to switch to a Convention case from a transition case must start from the beginning because the requirements have changed and the old forms cannot be converted into the new ones. Also, every country that signed the Convention has rules of its own.

If you would like to know if your case qualifies as a transition case, contact the Office of Children's Issue of the Department of State at AdoptionUSCA@state.gov, or call 888-407-4747 from the United States or Canada and 202-501-4444 outside the United States or Canada.

☆ ☆ ☆

I HOPE THAT ONE DAY I CAN HELP

MY FIRST FAMILY had a lot of children and couldn't take care of me. A lady from New York found me through an agency and decided to adopt me. It took a few years to work out. In the meantime, I was sent to live in a kind of orphanage where they weren't very nice to me. But every time my new mom came to see me, we stayed in a beautiful hotel together and got to know each other. I love her very much and I hope that, one day, I can help a child the way my mom helped me.

—Luisa, from Paraguay

CHAPTER 8

Paths to a Green Card: Employment, Investors

YOU MAY WANT TO APPLY for a green card because you are a foreign national with a job waiting for you in the United States. Or you may be an employer in the United States who wants to offer a job to someone in another country who will move here and become a green card holder. Most employers must file **Form ETA-750** with the U.S. Department of Labor to prove that a business has no choice but to hire an alien because no U.S. citizen or permanent resident can do a particular job. Exceptions are usually made for workers in categories EB-l and EB-2.

Workers in four categories may receive permanent resident visas.

◆ Priority workers (category EB-1, employment-based first preference)
In this category, the CIS includes workers with "extraordinary" ability in the sciences, arts, education, business, or athletics.

See the USCIS website: Immigration through Employment

They include prize winners, artists known around the world, or athletes competing for U.S. teams. Also listed here are "outstanding" professors and researchers, as well as managers and executives whose companies are transferring them from a foreign country to the United States.

◆ Professionals with graduate degrees or exceptional ability (category EB-2, employment-based second preference)
This category includes applicants with talents in the sciences, arts, or business, professionals with advanced degrees (such as doctorates or law degrees), and qualified doctors who will practice in areas of the United States that need doctors.

◆ Skilled or professional workers (EB-3, employment-based third preference)
Professionals with bachelor's degrees, skilled workers (those with at least two years of training and experience), and unskilled workers are in this category.

◆ Special immigrants (EB-4, employment-based fourth preference)
You are "special" if you work for a religious organization or if you worked in another country for the U.S. government.

◆ Some occupations are listed as Schedule A by the Department of Labor and certifications are usually granted for them. The occupations are physical therapists, professional nurses, and people of "exceptional ability" in the sciences or arts.

The Petition Process

1. As an employee or as an employer, you must be sure that the applicant for a green card is eligible for immigration through employment.

2. **Form ETA 750:** In most cases, the employer must complete a labor certification request (Form ETA 750) for the applicant (the employee). This must be submitted to the Department of Labor, Employment and Training Administration. The department will rule on the request by granting or denying it.

3. **Form I-140:** After the Department of Labor grants certification (in other words, approves ETA 750), an employer who wants to bring an applicant to the United States to work must file form I-140, Petition for Alien Worker. The employer is the sponsor (also called the petitioner) for the applicant who wants to permanently live and work in the United States. Form I-140 must be filed at a CIS service center.

   Each of the worker categories has its own rules for filing. The instructions with Form I-140 (and the other forms) explain exactly what must be done.

4. **Form I-360:** Workers who are classified as EB-4 or their employers must file form I-360, Petition for Amerasian, Widow(er), or Special Immigrant. The form has details on how to file it.

5. **Visa Number:** The U.S. Department of State gives the applicant an immigrant visa number. This happens even if the applicant is already in the United States. Receiving a visa number means that the applicant has been assigned an immigrant visa. But the visa process is far from over. (For information about receiving the Visa Bulletin, see Appendix B.)

6. Once a visa number becomes available, the applicant who is in this country must complete the process for getting a green card.

   Applicants outside the United States who are notified that their visa number is available must complete the green card process at their local U.S. consulates.

Doctors Needed

Foreign doctors may be sent to areas where the U.S. Department of Health and Human Services sees a need for physicians. Such immigrants don't have to submit form ETA 750 to the Department of Labor. Nor do doctors who will work in facilities that officially care for veterans.

☆ ☆ ☆

I WAS VERY FORTUNATE

IT TOOK ME more than 12 years, but I did finally get my green card. I was very fortunate. It didn't matter to me [how long it took] since I was already here on assignment for my government on a business visa. Now, though, I have a great job at a hotel and I can stay forever.

—Imelda, from the Philippines

☆ ☆ ☆

WELCOME TO AMERICA!

I APPLIED FOR my green card as an artist with "exceptional abilities." (I'm a cartoonist.) It took me eight months to collect all the materials needed to fulfill the requirements (samples of my works, exhibitions, reviews, BFA papers, letters of recommendation, and proof that the people giving those letters were qualified).

Once my wife Andrea and I put everything together in two binders with about 100 pages each, I gave the material to the lawyer who sent it to immigration. She [the lawyer] said to expect an answer in from six to eight months.

She got everything back in two months and thought, "Oh, there must be something wrong. It was sent back!" When she opened the package, she was surprised to see that my application was approved!

I went to have my interview a few months later in Ciudad Juarez in Mexico, across from El Paso, Texas. Everything went fine and the immigration people even asked me to draw a cartoon at the time of the interview! Later, after showing my papers at the border, the officer told me "Welcome to America!" It felt so great!

—Felipe, from Mexico

Investors

USCIS website: Immigration through Investment

If you have at least $500,000 to invest in an American business, immigration as an investor may be for you. Every year, 10,000 visas are set aside for investors, people who can prove that they are creating, building up, and investing in commercial enterprises—in other words, businesses that make money—in the United States. These visas are called EB-5 visas.

Eligible businesses must help improve the United States economy. In most areas, investors must have $1 million to build a business. This money must have been earned lawfully. In specific areas with longtime high unemployment rates, the investment must be at least $500,000. To be eligible, investors must provide—directly or indirectly—ten or more full time jobs and/or generate increased exports.

To be eligible for the EB-5 visa, investors must be ready to take an active part after doing at least one of these things:

◆ starting a new business
◆ buying an existing business and then reorganizing it so that a new business results
◆ expanding an existing business that is in trouble—that has, for example, lost 20% of its net worth over the past year or two

Half of the EB-5, or 5,000, visas go to investors who take part in a program called Regional Center. (This is a pilot program, which means it is being tested and may not last forever.) A Regional Center deals mainly with certain areas of the United States and hopes to create new jobs, increase export sales, and improve productivity in those areas by aiding economic growth.

Rules Change

Given the uncertain state of the U.S. economy, these rules about immigration for investors may change. People seeking EB-5 visas must first check with the USCIS.

Forms You Will Need

1. **Form I-526:** If you are eligible to be an immigrant investor, you must first file Form I-526, the Immigrant Petition by Alien Entrepreneur. This form must be sent with documents that prove your investment meets all requirements.
2. **Form I-485:** To become a conditional resident after Form I-526 is approved, eligible investors must file Form I-485, Application to Register Permanent Residence or Adjust Status.
3. **Form I-829:** To become a lawful permanent resident, you must file Form I-829, Petition by Entrepreneur to Remove Conditions. Form I-829 must be filed within 90 days of the second anniversary of your admission to the United States as a conditional resident.

Amnesties

Certain people may be given an amnesty—in other words, they may be forgiven for breaking immigration laws. In a recent amnesty, the United States forgave aliens who had been in this country since January 1, 1982. People from Nicaragua, Cuba, Guatemala, El Salvador, and some Eastern European countries also qualified for amnesties. The law that helped them is called the Immigration Reform and Control Act of 1986.

Important Warning: If you are illegal, don't ask the USCIS about amnesties. You may risk being deported. Get advice from a lawyer.

CHAPTER 9

Paths to a Green Card: Refugees and Asylum Seekers

[A refugee] is a person who has fled his or her country of origin because of past persecution or a well-founded fear of persecution based upon race, religion, nationality, political opinion, or a membership in a particular social group.

—U.S. law

EVERY YEAR, the horror of being persecuted causes millions of people around the world to flee their homelands. They face threats, violence, bullying, and discrimination. You may have suffered such conditions, which is why you fear returning home. Now you may be able to come to the United States as a refugee or asylum seeker (asylee) and live here for as long as you want. By resettling in the United States, you and your family will be in a strange place living among strangers. But your life should be peaceful and safe.

The basic difference between a refugee and an asylee is where you are when you apply to enter the United States. A person who is outside his

See the USCIS website: Eligibility: Who May Apply to Be Resettled in the United States as a Refugee?

or her country, but not in the United States, is a refugee. A person who is at the border or inside the United States is an asylee.

It is not easy to be admitted as a refugee. The U.S. government sets a limit on the number of refugees it will admit and where they come from. (This is called "setting a quota.") In 2005, for example, the number was set at 70,000 from six areas of the world: Africa, East Asia, Latin America and the Caribbean, the Near East, and South Asia

When you seek refugee status, you must prove that you were persecuted. Without documents or witnesses, that's a difficult thing to do. But it can be done. You have to tell your story in a way it is believed. You don't have to be an actor, simply someone who is honestly recounting details of terrible events that caused you to flee. Details should include as many names, dates, and places as you can remember. You can include letters from doctors to prove you were tortured or that you were subject to female genital cutting. You can try to supply newspaper articles that mention you or what has happened to people like you in your country.

Being eligible for refugee status doesn't mean you will definitely be resettled in the United States. You might not be admitted if you

◆ have certain diseases that are catching (communicable).
◆ are a security risk.
◆ have been involved in terrorist activity.
◆ abuse drugs or broke laws about controlled substances.
◆ have been resettled in another country.
◆ committed two or more criminal offenses.
◆ ordered or took part in persecution.
◆ have committed serious crimes, but were given immunity.
◆ plan to practice polygamy in the United States.
◆ have been involved in international child abduction.
◆ will cause an international incident if you are admitted.

The secretary of Homeland Security can make exceptions for some of these rules.

To find out if you are eligible for resettlement in the United States, you must get in touch with the United Nations High Commissioner for Refugees (UNHCR) or your nearest U.S. embassy or consulate. A refugee resettlement agency in the United States could also help you if you have U.S. relatives who can get in touch with it.

To try for refugee status, you must file the following forms. A refugee organization will probably help you find and fill out these forms.

◆ Form **I-590**, Registration for Classification as Refugee
◆ some proof of persecution or an affidavit that shows why you should be classified as a refugee
◆ Form **G-325C**, Biographical Information for anyone over 14 years old
◆ Form **I-134**, Affidavit of Support—your sponsor can be a person or a group
◆ medical exam report

Your spouse (husband or wife) and unmarried children under 21 years old must be with you at your refugee interview to receive refugee status. If they aren't with you when you are interviewed, they will be allowed to follow you to the United States. But you will have to file **Form I-730**, Refugee/Asylee Relative Petition, for each of them. Each must be eligible for admission.

After the USCIS approves your application, agencies not connected with the government take over the process. They will get in touch with your relatives in the United States to find out about your jobs and skills. They will ask about educational and medical needs you and your immediate family may have. That will help with deciding where to resettle you. The agencies will also interview you, help prepare your documents for the USCIS, set up security checks, and arrange medical exams.

Once you receive refugee status, you will be given a parole visa. You have four months to enter the United States. The International Organization for Migration (IOM) sets up transportation to the

United States for refugees. The cost can be repaid after you are settled in your new home. You can also set up your own transportation.

When you first arrive, an agent from a resettlement agency will meet you and help you to start your new life. You may go to live near your relatives, or you may be sent to a town or city anywhere in the United States. As soon as you enter, you will be allowed to look for work. This can be a time of discovery and excitement for you and your family. The important thing is to welcome good new experiences. In the past 20 years, two million refugees have settled in this country. Most have found it to be a real refuge and have made a smooth passage from one life into another.

Applying for political asylum may be slightly more complicated. You can request asylum

◆ when you arrive at the United States border or at a port of entry (but you cannot be a ship or plane crew member or a passenger in transit from one flight to another).

◆ at a hearing for your deportation (removal).

◆ by applying to the USCIS even if you are here illegally.

If you ask for asylum at the border or at a port of entry, you will be sent before an immigration judge to make your case. If you possibly can, now is a good time to get the help of a lawyer. You will have to file the following list of documents. Send them to your nearest USCIS Regional Service Center (see Appendix B) or, if you are in removal hearings, to the Immigration Court.

◆ **Form I-589**, Application for Asylum and for Withholding of Removal. File the original and two copies.

◆ one color passport-style photo of you and each relative who is applying with you. Lightly write your name on the back in pencil.

◆ three copies of passports or I-94 card

◆ three copies of proof of identity, such as a birth certificate or national ID document

◆ three copies of documents that prove the relationship between you and your relatives, such as birth and marriage certificates

◆ three copies of your statement and papers to support why you were forced to leave your homeland

◆ three copies of statements from people from your homeland supporting your statement

A few weeks after the USCIS has processed your documents, you will be called to the USCIS Asylum Office for an interview. If your English isn't strong, you may want to take along a translator. This should be a person who is very fluent in and comfortable speaking English. The questions asked will be sharp and probing and even surprising.

In less than six months or so, you will be told if you have received asylum. If you have, you'll be given a paper stating this. If you are denied asylum, you will have to appear in Immigration Court. You can then appeal the decision. In the meantime, you can stay in the United States. One year after being admitted into the United States as a refugee or being granted asylum, it's time to apply for adjustment to permanent resident status (the green card).

Refugees must apply for their green cards after one year.

☆ ☆ ☆

THE WHEELS TURN SLOWLY

SHORTLY AFTER I applied for American citizenship, I misplaced my green card. I applied for a new one. I knew that I didn't need the actual card in hand, but I liked having it. I waited and waited. In the meantime, I worked at getting my citizenship. About a week after I was sworn in as a U.S. citizen, my new green card arrived in the mail! The wheels of the government turn slowly.

—Rachel, from Israel

Asylees are eligible to apply, but don't have to. The USCIS, however, advises that you do. One reason is that a limited number of asylees receive green cards in a year, so your application may be delayed for a year or more. In the meantime, conditions in your homeland may get better. The USCIS may then decide that you no longer need asylum and may decide to send you home. Until you get your green card, you will have to renew your work permit from year to year.

You can travel outside the United States while your Form I-485 is being processed. You just need a Refugee Travel Document to return. To apply for this, you need another form, Form I-131, Application for Travel Document. Give yourself plenty of time to have your papers ready. It takes 150 days before you begin travel to receive this document.

Your spouse or child (called "derivative asylees") filing for an adjustment to permanent resident status must prove that their situation is unchanged. Your husband or wife must still be married to you. Your child must still be under 21 and unmarried. When they file, they must give your A (alien) number as well as:

◆ proof of the relationship
◆ copies of the letters that gave them derivative asylee status because they were included on your original asylum application, or
◆ Form I-797 showing that they are approved beneficiaries of an I-730 petition that you filed

What happens to your child if he or she is now over 21 years old or married? You must get in touch with the nearest asylum office. Ask for information on filing Form I-589 for an asylum application called a *nunc pro tunc*. The child can then apply for adjustment of status after being in the United States for one year after the date asylum was granted.

Asylees: Forms You Will Need and Steps to Take

1. File **Form I-485**, Application to Register Permanent Residence or to Adjust Status. Carefully follow the instructions on the form.

2. Prepare a separate I-485 application packet for yourself (the principal applicant) and for your husband or wife and each child who received derivative asylee or refugee status from you.
3. You may mail all the application packets together, but each family unit's packet should be identified.

Example: Suppose there are two family units, the Smiths and the Asantes. All the packets for the Smith family should be held together by one rubber band. All the packets of the Asante family should be held together by another rubber band.

4. An expert English translation should go along with any documents you send that are in a foreign language. See Chapter 6 for a form that the translator should use. A clear and readable copy of the original document must go along with the translation.
5. You must send the following materials with your I-485—in the order listed:
   ➤ fingerprint fee (only applicants from 14 to 78 years old need to pay)
   ➤ I-485 filing fee
      If you use one check to pay for all the applications, attach the check to the top left-hand corner of the first form in the packet. If you use a separate check for each application, attach it to the top left-hand corner of each appropriate application.

      Very Important: If you send one check for all applications and it is in the wrong amount, all the applications will be sent back. Separate checks are better.
   ➤ **G-28** if it applies to you. Your lawyer or representative and you, the applicant, must sign this. Your lawyer or representatives may use signature stamps. But you must sign the original of the form submitted.
   ➤ **Form I-485**, signed. Box d of Part 2 of the application should be marked. If you are an Iraqi who went through Guam, also write "Iraqi/Guam" in the margin.

> two photos stapled to the lower left corner of an envelope. Lightly write your name and A number, if you know it, in pencil on the back of each photo. Then, if they are separated, they won't get lost.

> evidence of your asylee status. You might include a copy of **Form I-94** and a clear, readable copy of the letter granting you asylum. If you first got conditional asylum, include proof that the conditions were removed.

> **Form I-602**, Application by Refugee for Waiver on Grounds of Excludability. Send only if it applies to you.

> proof that you were in the United States for one year. You might include a letter of employment, an apartment lease, school records, or any document that provides a record of the entire year.

> proof of any times you were out of the country since you were granted asylum. You could send copies of pages in a travel document or in your passport.

> birth certificate or birth record

> proof of any legal name change since you received asylum

> **Form I-693**, report of medical examination and vaccination record

Call the USCIS at 800-375-5283 to find doctors in your area who are allowed to perform the exams. In the language of the USCIS, these doctors are called "civil surgeons."

To hold this material together, use one staple or a large paper clip.

To find out how long it may take your case to be completed, call USCIS customer service at 800-375-5283. You will need your A number, receipt numbers, and the last notice you were sent about your case. The USCIS warns that dates can never be exact. Delays happen.

Refugees: Forms You Will Need and Steps to Take

You must send the following materials with your **I-485**—in the order listed: (To hold this material together, use one staple or a large paper clip.)

◆ fingerprint fee (only applicants from 14 to 78 years old need to pay)

If you use one check to pay for all the applications, attach the check to the top left-hand corner of the first form in the packet. If you use a separate check for each application, attach each one to the top left-hand corner of the appropriate application.

Very Important: If you send one check for all applications and it is in the wrong amount, all the applications will be sent back. It is better to use separate checks.

◆ Form I-485, signed. In box h of Part 2, print the word "refugee" on the line.

◆ two photos stapled to the lower left corner of an envelope. Lightly write your name and A number, if you know it, in pencil on the back of each photo. Then, if they are separated, they won't get lost.

◆ G-28 if it applies to you. This must be signed by your lawyer or representative and by you, the applicant. Your lawyer or representatives may use signature stamps. But you must sign, in ink, the original of the form submitted.

◆ Vaccination supplemental form to **I-693**. A complete Form I-693 (which includes Form I-693 and its supplement) is needed only if you faced being rejected on medical grounds when you arrived or if you were granted refugee status by an approved **Form I-730**. Call the USCIS at 800-375-5283 to find doctors in your area who can vaccinate you. In the language of the USCIS, these doctors are called "civil surgeons."

◆ proof of your refugee status. You might include a copy of **Form I-94** and a clear, readable copy of the letter granting you refugee status. If you first received conditional asylum, include proof that the conditions were removed.

◆ **Form I-602**, Application by Refugee for Waiver on Grounds of Excludability, only if it applies to you.

◆ proof that you have been in the United States for one year. You might include a letter of employment, an apartment lease, school records, or any document that provides a record of the entire year.

◆ proof of any times you were out of the country since you were granted asylum. You could send copies of pages in a travel document or in your passport.

◆ birth certificate or birth record

◆ proof of any legal name change since you received asylum

Where to File Your Documents

If you are an asylee applying for an adjustment of status, your adjustment of status applications must be sent to one of two service centers, depending on where you live.

If you live in:

Alaska

Arizona

California

Colorado

Guam

Hawaii

Idaho

Illinois

Indiana

Iowa

Kansas

Michigan

Minnesota

Missouri

Montana

Nebraska

Nevada

North Dakota

Ohio
Oregon
South Dakota
Utah
Washington
Wisconsin
Wyoming

Use this mailing address:
USCIS
Nebraska Service Center
P.O. Box 87485
Lincoln, NE 68501-7485

If you live in:
Alabama
Arkansas
Connecticut
Delaware
Florida
Georgia
Kentucky
Louisiana
Maine
Maryland
Massachusetts
Mississippi
New Hampshire
New Jersey
New Mexico
New York
North Carolina
South Carolina
Oklahoma
Pennsylvania

Puerto Rico
Rhode Island
Tennessee
Texas
Vermont
Virginia
U.S. Virgin Islands
West Virginia
Washington, D.C.

Use this mailing address:
USCIS
Texas Service Center
P.O. Box 852211
Mesquite, TX 75185-2211

If you are a refugee applying for an adjustment of status, all applications should be sent to:
USCIS
Nebraska Service Center
P.O. Box 87209
Lincoln, NE 68501-7209

Agencies That Resettle Refugees

The United States has 10 agencies that resettle refugees nationwide on behalf of the U.S. government. They are:

Church World Service
CWS Immigration and Refugee Program headquarters
475 Riverside Drive, Suite 700
New York, NY 10115
Phone: 212-870-3300
Fax: 212-870-2132
www.churchworldservice.org

Ethiopian Community Development Council
901 South Highland Street
Arlington, Virginia 22204
Phone: 703-685-0510
Fax: 703-685-0529
E-mail: info@ecdcinternational

Episcopal Migration Ministries
815 Second Avenue
New York, NY 10017
Phone: 212-716-6000 or 800-334-7626
www.episcopalchurch.org/emm/

Hebrew Immigrant Aid Society
333 Seventh Avenue, 16th Floor
New York, NY 10001-5004
Phone: 212-216-7697 or 800-HIAS-714
Fax: 212-967-4483
www.hias.org

Iowa Department of Human Services
(Iowa only)
1200 University Avenue, Suite D
Des Moines, IA 50314
Phone: 515-283-7999 or 800-362-2780
Fax: 515-283-9160
refugee@dhs.state.ia.us

International Rescue Committee
122 East 42nd Street
New York, NY 10168
Phone: 212-551-3000
www.theirc.org

Lutheran Immigration and Refugee Service

122 C Street, NW, Suite 125

Washington DC 20001

Phone: 202-783-7509

Fax: 202-783-7502

www.lirs.org

U.S. Committee for Refugees and Immigrants

2231 Crystal Drive, Suite 350

Arlington, VA 22202-3711

Phone: 703-310-1130

Fax: 703-769-4241

www.refugees.org

United States Conference of Catholic Bishops/Migration and Refugee Services

3211 Fourth Street NE

Washington, DC 20017

Phone: 202-541-3170

Fax: 202-722-8750

mrsrp@usccb.org

World Relief

7 East Baltimore St

Baltimore MD 21202

Phone: 443-451-1900 or 800-535-5433

worldrelief@wr.org

TPS

People who flee civil wars or natural disasters are given Temporary Protected Status (TPS), which usually lasts up to 18 months. It doesn't lead to a green card.

CHAPTER 10

Paths to a Green Card: Registry, Special Immigrants, Iraqi or Afghan Translators, Private Bills Registry

EVEN IF YOU are an undocumented alien—illegally in this country—you may still become a lawful permanent resident. This is because of the registry provisions that are part of immigration law.

You may be eligible for a green card as part of the registry provisions if you

◆ entered the United States before January 1, 1972
◆ have always lived here since you arrived
◆ are of "good moral character"

See the USCIS website: How Do I Apply for Admission . . . Under the Registry Provision?

◆ are eligible for citizenship
◆ never took part in genocide (murder of a group of people belonging to the same ethnic group)

Proving that you have been here for the required amount of time. The USCIS won't just take your word for it. You have to prove that you came before 1972 and that you've lived in this country continually (without interruption). Along with **Form I-485**, Application to Register Permanent Residence or Adjust Status, you must submit documents to prove what you are claiming. Here are a few of the documents that will help you make your case.

◆ credit card statements, loan statements
◆ electric, gas, and telephone bills
◆ official birth, death, or marriage certificates for you or your immediate family
◆ passport, form I-94, and any other documents that show when you arrived here
◆ driver's license or any other license issued by the government for your car or business, for example
◆ bank statements
◆ letters with clear postmarks addressed to you
◆ pay stubs or other job-related paperwork
◆ medical and dental records
◆ dated photos of important events in which you took part
◆ statements from people, including religious leaders and employers, saying that you have been here since 1972

What is Good Moral Character?

This book is about how to get a green card. But a small number of people need to be told why they are *not* eligible for a green card. These are people who would not be good or lawful permanent residents. A person is *not* of good moral character if he or she has:

(continues)

> ➤ committed an aggravated felony (includes violent crimes that involve at least a one-year prison term)
> ➤ committed a murder
> ➤ taken part in terrorist acts
> ➤ committed a rape
> ➤ attacked a child
> ➤ taken part in illegal trade of drugs, firearms, or people
> ➤ committed a crime in which a victim was robbed or defrauded, where someone was physically harmed or threatened.

Which Forms You'll Need and What Steps to Take

◆ **Form I-485** and **Form G-325A** Send I-485 with a filing fee and completed form G-325A with proof that you have always lived in the United States since your arrival. You must prove that you are eligible for the granting of registry. (See the list.)

◆ Send your forms to the USCIS district office that is in charge of the place where you live. (For locations, see the listing in Appendix A.)

Example 1: If you live in Holbrooke, New York, your local office is in New York City at the Jacob Javits Federal Building 26 Federal Plaza, 3rd Floor, Room 3-310, New York, NY 10278.

Example 2: If you live in San Diego, California, your local office is at 880 Front Street, San Diego, CA 92101. The Chula Vista Field Office also serves this area and is located at 1261 3rd Avenue, Suite A, Chula Vista, CA 91911.

◆ The USCIS website is extremely helpful in this instance. Go to USCIS Service and Office Locator on the computer. You just need to know your zip code in order to find the address of your local office.

◆ If the district director says you are not eligible to apply under the registry provision, you cannot appeal. But you can apply again before an immigration judge.

Special Immigrants

If you are serving in the U.S. military and recently became a citizen, you can upgrade your spouse, unmarried minor children, and your parents to the status of immediate relative. To do this, you will first have to file Form I-130, Petition for Alien Relative. If this form is already pending, call the USCIS Military Help Line, 1-877-CIS-4MIL (247-4645), to request that the USCIS upgrade your relative's visa category to immediate relative status.

If you are serving in the U.S. military but are a legal permanent resident, your spouse and unmarried minor children aren't considered immediate relatives and will have to wait. But if you filed a Form I-130 for your spouse, he or she may be eligible for a V-l nonimmigrant visa. This must be filed at a U.S. consulate overseas. At the same time, Forms DS-3052 and DS-156, nonimmigrant visa applications, must be filed with the U.S. Department of State. But this is not a guarantee that your spouse will qualify for the V-l visa.

If he or she does, though, your spouse will be allowed into the United States to adjust status to lawful permanent resident when his or her immigrant visa number becomes available.

If you are a U.S. citizen and have filed Form I-129F, Petition for Alien Fiance(é), for your spouse, you may ask the USCIS to speed up the processing of the petition by calling the Military Help Line. If you are outside the United States, you can mail the forms to the USCIS Service Center listed on the Form I-129F instructions. (A lawful permanent resident cannot file a Form 129-F.)

After USCIS approves the Form I-129F, your fiancé(e) may file an application for a K-1 nonimmigrant visa at a U.S. Consulate overseas. A K-1 visa allows your fiancé(e) to enter the United States only to marry you. You must marry within 90 days of his or her admission or the K-1 visa will expire. If you marry, your new spouse may file to become a lawful permanent resident by filing Form I-485, Application to Register Permanent Residence or Adjust Status.

☆ ☆ ☆

I MAY BE THE OLDEST LIVING GREEN CARD HOLDER . . .

I HAVE HAD a green card for at least 50 years, since shortly after I moved to the United States from Belgium with my husband. Belgium doesn't offer dual citizenship as, for example, France does. I never could bring myself to give up my Belgian citizenship even though I hardly ever return there. So I have kept my green card. My grandchildren say I may be the oldest living green card holder in the country!

—Elisabet, from Belgium

Iraqi or Afghan Translators for the U.S. Armed Forces

The good news for nationals of Iraq or Afghanistan who worked with the U.S. Armed Forces is that they can get visas to come to the United States. The not-so-good news is that only 50 translators are eligible each year for this special immigration visa. For 2008 only, the government raised the number of translators eligible for an immigration visa to 500. It's always possible that may happen again. To be eligible, you

- ◆ must have worked directly with the U.S. Armed Forces or under Chief of Mission authority as a translator or interpreter for at least 12 months
- ◆ must have received a written recommendation from a general or flag officer in your unit from the embassy where you worked
- ◆ must have passed a background check and screening
- ◆ must be eligible to receive a regular immigrant visa and be admissible to the United States for permanent residence

To get the process going, file **Form I-360** with the USCIS Nebraska Service Center.

Private Bills

If you have tried every path you could to stay in the United States and avoid being deported, you have one chance left. It isn't going to be easy, though. To have a bill passed on your behalf by the U.S. Congress, your story must be so compelling and the injustice against you so awful that more than one important American politician must be willing to fight on your behalf. Since 1996, 500 private bills have been introduced, but only 36 were passed. Many were efforts to keep families together.

More than one member of the U.S. House of Representatives and more than one senator have to push for you to receive permanent residency or even citizenship. Committees in both houses of Congress have to agree with them. Then, during a regular legislative session, the private bill must be voted on and approved by both houses. And then the president of the United States must sign it into law.

CHAPTER 11

Paths to a Green Card: Diversity Visa Lottery Winners

EVERY YEAR, the Department of State makes 55,000 immigrant visas available through the Diversity Visa Lottery (DV) program. The lottery is for people who come from countries that don't send many immigrants to the United States. (The word "diversity" means *variety* or *mixture*. The lottery is meant to bring in many different kinds of people to this country.)

In 2008, the DV received 6.4 million applications—up from 5.5 million the year before. So it's clear that no one should depend on winning the lottery to get a green card. In fact, just because you are a lottery winner doesn't mean you'll get a green card. You must move quickly so you get your card while they're still available. You must go through the immigration process and receive your card by September 30 of the year just after you win. This has been a problem in the past.

See the USCIS website: Diversity Lottery.

Example: People who applied in 2009 will be notified in 2010 and must complete the immigration process by September 30, 2010. Because the Department of State and the CIS work very slowly, lottery winners have missed their big chance.

Here's how the Diversity Visa Lottery is supposed to work: The Department of State chooses about 55,000 random (with no particular plan or pattern) applications from all those that were filed and are eligible. When the 55,000 are chosen or the government's fiscal year ends, the lottery is over for the year.

The lottery cannot be entered through the USCIS website and applications should not be filed with the USCIS, as most other visa applications are. The electronic Diversity Visa entry form can be downloaded from the Department of State site. Successful lottery applicants receive a letter from the Department of State telling them of their luck. Successful applicants are never notified by e-mail.

Example: The 2010 lottery started online at 12:00 noon Eastern Daylight Time (EDT) on October 2, 2008. It ended at 12:00 noon Eastern Daylight Time (EDT) on December 1, 2008.

The Kentucky Consular Center in Williamsburg, which is in charge of the lottery, gives numbers to the entries in the order it receives them. The earlier an applicant applies, the lower the number of the entry. When entries are chosen, the Department of State gives entrants a chance to apply for immigration visas.

Don't Get Cheated

Never pay someone to submit an application to the Diversity Visa Lottery. No one can improve your chances to win. Don't believe anyone who promises prizes like plane tickets in addition to visas, no matter how trustworthy the person claims to be.

☆ ☆ ☆

BE PATIENT

I TRIED the lottery four or five times, but ended up getting my green card just by applying. My advice is to keep trying. Two of my friends did get their cards after winning the lottery. Be patient, it is a very, very long process.

—Yuk Pang, from China

Following Up Your Status Online

You need an application receipt number to check the status of your case online.

CHAPTER 12

Important Questions and Answers

1. Do green cards automatically lead to citizenship?
No. You must apply for citizenship and, in most cases, go through the naturalization process.

2. What is the difference between a visa and a green card?
The government uses the term visa most often when talking about numbers and quotas. You need an immigrant visa to enter this country before applying for a green card. A green card shows that you are a lawful, *permanent* resident of the United States.

3. How long will it take to get my green card?
After the terrorist attacks of September 11, 2001, stricter rules about immigration to the United States went into effect. These have made getting a visa a longer and more complicated process. The government

is trying to make the process move more quickly, but it still gets delayed.

> *Example: In 2008 the USCIS and the Federal Bureau of Investigation (FBI) decided to end name checks on applications that had been submitted more than two years ago. What does this mean to you? Checking to make sure names are real takes time. It was one reason hundreds of thousands of applicants had such long waits. Almost 350,000 applicants were waiting for a name check in 2007. In 2008, this number was cut to less than 37,000. By 2009, the FBI hoped to take care of all name checks that were more than six months old.*

Every year, the U.S. Congress sets a limit on the number of visas allowed. **Visa numbers** are given out based on preference and priority number. Still, you may not receive your immigrant visa number right away even if the USCIS has approved your visa petition. It's possible that you could wait more than a year for your visa number. If you come from a country that has many people going to the United States— China, India, Mexico, and the Philippines, for example—your wait could be much longer.

Some people may be lucky enough to avoid a long wait. If you are an immediate relative (see Chapter 5), you only have to wait for your application to work its way through the process. This may take from two months to a year. Once the process is complete, a visa is yours.

Your consulate or embassy may be able to let you know how long your process will take. The best advice for everyone: Submit your visa application as soon as you can.

4. What is the Visa Bulletin?

It is published by the Department of State and gives you the month and year of the visa petitions it is working on. They are listed by country and preference category. You can figure out from this information about how long it could take you to get your visa number. To do that, look under your country's name and your category.

*Example: Suppose the Department of State is working on applica-
tions with priority dates of January 2002. Your priority date is July
2006. This means you may have to wait several years for your immigrant visa number.*

5. What is the difference between a "conditional" and a "permanent" resident?

Conditional residents have the same rights and responsibilities as permanent residents do. (See Chapter 2.) But they must file **Form I-751**
before they can become permanent residents.

If a husband and wife have been married for less than two years at
the time one spouse gets a green card, the couple must apply together
90 days before the two years are up to the Department of Homeland
Security to remove the conditional status. (Yes. Here's a case of being
permanent and conditional.) The conditional resident must file **Form
I-751**, Petition to Remove the Conditions on Residence. When this
condition is approved, the immigrant spouse will receive a permanent
residence card (green card).

Immigrants who are investors (EB-5) also have conditional visas for
two years and must apply after that for their permanent residence.
Form I-829, Petition by Entrepreneur to Remove Conditions, must be
filed within two years of the date the investors, or entrepreneurs,
became conditional permanent residents.

The two-year date is the date that the permanent resident card
expires. Conditional permanent residents must file their forms within
90 days of the two-year anniversary of when they got their conditional
resident status. Not doing this may mean losing immigration status. To
be ready for the 90-day date means gathering documents and information in time.

6. What does it mean to "maintain a residence?"

This is also called maintaining a domicile. A sponsor must have his or
her main home permanently in the United States before the USCIS will
grant a visa. Some exceptions exist.

7. What makes an applicant ineligible for a visa?

Some reasons a person may not be given a visa are: drug trafficking, having HIV/AIDS, overstaying a previous visa, being a polygamist, supporting the overthrow of the U.S. government, and filing fake documents. For complete information, see http://www.travel.state.gov/visa/frvi/ineligibilities/ineligibilities_1364.html.

8. What is a "fraud interview?"

The U.S. government knows that some marriages take place just so one partner can get a green card. So, before your application for permanent resident status is approved, the USCIS wants to talk to you and your spouse. If you take along reliable proof that you are well and truly married and your answers are honest, the interview should be easy. If, however, you don't have the right documents and the USCIS believes you have a "paper marriage," things will be tougher.

In 1986, because there were so many paper marriages, the U.S. Congress passed the Immigration Marriage Fraud Amendments. These laws made it a federal crime to take part in a marriage meant only to help in immigration. People caught doing this face fines of $250,000, jail time, and removal (deportation). And forget about ever getting a green card.

If the USCIS thinks you are in a paper marriage, it will put you and your spouse through a fraud interview. Each of you will be in a separate room, but asked the same questions. If your answers don't match, that is probably the end of your hopes as an immigrant.

Examples of documents to prove a real marriage: marriage certificate, wedding photos, rental or home purchase agreements. (See Chapter 6.)

9. What is "premium processing?"

For a $1,000 fee (in 2009), certain green card applicants can get their processing done faster by using the Premium Processing Service from the USCIS. Processing of employment-based petitions and applications will be done in 15 days. If this sounds too good to be true, it is—for most people. It is mainly available to businesses that want to bring important employees to the United States. The USCIS will refund the fee if processing is not done in the 15 days that were promised. The case, though, will continue to be processed. The 15-day period begins when the USCIS receives **Form I-907**, Request for Premium Processing Service, filled out correctly.

In the past, there have been a quite a few cases of fraud involving people trying to use this service. So the USCIS is especially careful in granting it. The website has a complete chart of exactly who is eligible. Go to www.uscis.gov/premiumprocessing for more information.

10. Do I need a work permit?

Yes, if you aren't a permanent resident—that is, if you don't have your green card, but are waiting for one. If you live in the United States and have filed **Form-465**, Application to Register Permanent Residence or Adjust Status, you can get a work permit while you wait for your application to go through. To get a work permit, you must file **Form I-765**.

11. How do I file my forms and other documents?

Most documents have to be filed by mail. After you make copies (see question 13), take the sealed envelope to the post office and send it certified mail return receipt requested. This means someone will have to sign for your package when it arrives and you can track it. Keep the receipt in a safe place with your other copies.

You can file some applications online. This is called e-filing. When you use it, you can pay your fees with a credit card and find out right away that the USCIS has received your documents. But you still have to use regular mail to send copies of your documents. And, if you make a mistake with your fees, you won't get a refund. The USCIS is still working on this idea.

Every form comes with detailed instructions (some are 10 pages long) about where and how to mail it.

Before mailing your paperwork, check that you've done all of the following.

_____ Carefully read the instructions with the forms.

_____ Written your entire name. *Example: Laura Emily O'Neill*

_____ Made sure your written name matches the name on your birth certificate.

_____ Answered all the questions truthfully.

_____ Included the right fees.

_____ Included all the documents that were requested. (Check twice.)

_____ Signed all papers that need a signature. Example: *Laura Emily O'Neill*

_____ Double-checked the mailing address.

12. May I leave the United States to visit my family?

Yes. But, of course, you must fill out the right form and follow the rules.

If you are waiting for your application to go through as part of the registry provision (see Chapter 10): Fill out **Form I-131**, have the CIS approve it, and receive advance parole. *Advance parole* means that, before you go, you have received permission to leave and return to the United States. Your registry application will still be okay when you get back. If you don't get advance parole, you may be kept out of the United States.

You also need advance parole if you are in these groups: K-1 visa, asylum applicants, people with Temporary Protected Status, and some people who are trying to change, or adjust, their status while they are here.

If you became a lawful permanent resident under the registry provision and will be away for six months or less, you do not have to apply for permission.

If you have a green card and leave for more than six months, you must reapply for permission at your port of entry.

13. Can my family from another country visit me if I am waiting for my green card?

Your family will have to get nonimmigrant visas or whatever the correct documents are for your country. But if one of your relatives has applied to become a green card holder, the U.S. embassy might not want to approve a nonimmigrant visa. It is important for everyone to tell the consul that he or she has an approved visa petition.

As with everything in life, exceptions are made.

Example 1: Your relative could appeal in person and make a strong case for getting a short-term visa.

Example 2: Husbands or wives of U.S. citizens may be eligible for a K visa.

Example 3: Temporary workers may qualify for an H or L visa.

14. Do I need a medical exam?

If you are applying for adjustment of status (see Chapter 14), you most likely will need a medical examination. (Some people do not need an exam. Check with the USCIS to find out if you do.) These exams are performed by people called civil surgeons who are doctors approved by the USCIS. You will need to file **Form I-485** with your exam results.

The USCIS has an easy-to-use site to find a doctor near you. Go to the Civil Surgeon Locator at http://www.uscis.gov/portal/site/uscis.

Applicants must also have their vaccinations up to date before they receive immigrant visas. Proof that you have the correct vaccinations comes from the doctors who perform the medical exams.

Here is a list of vaccinations that you may need. Just because a vaccination is on the list doesn't mean you will have to get it. It depends on your age and medical condition, and if you were vaccinated as a child. Your doctor will decide. It would help to have your medical records from your homeland. For more information, go to http://travel.state.gov/visa/immigrants/info/info_1339.html.

__ Acellular pertussis
__ Hepatitis A
__ Hepatitis B
__ Human papillomavirus (HPV)
__ Influenza

__ Influenza type b (Hib)

__ Measles

__ Meningococcal

__ Mumps

__ Pneumococcal

__ Pertussis

__ Polio

__ Rotovirus

__ Tetanus and diphtheria toxoids

__ Varicella

__ Zoster

15. How important is it to keep my own file?

Very, very important! You'll be dealing with a lot of people. Most will be working for different parts of the government. Each person will have a mountain of paperwork—yours and that of many others as well. You will be the only person who knows exactly what is going on with your application. Make sure that every piece of paper you submit, such as your photograph, has your name on it.

Applications sometimes get lost. That's why your best friend while you wait for your green card may be a copy machine or someone who has one. (Many personal printers also make copies. And most local libraries have public copy machines that can be used for a small charge.)

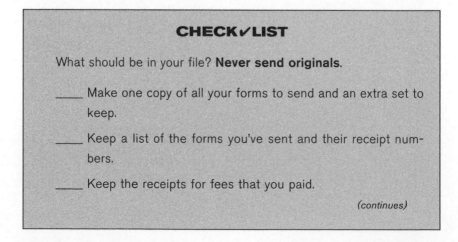

CHECK✓LIST

What should be in your file? **Never send originals.**

_____ Make one copy of all your forms to send and an extra set to keep.

_____ Keep a list of the forms you've sent and their receipt numbers.

_____ Keep the receipts for fees that you paid.

(continues)

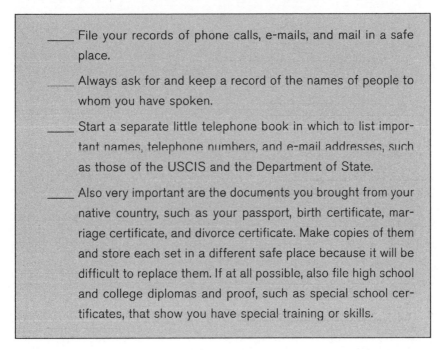

_____ File your records of phone calls, e-mails, and mail in a safe place.

_____ Always ask for and keep a record of the names of people to whom you have spoken.

_____ Start a separate little telephone book in which to list important names, telephone numbers, and e-mail addresses, such as those of the USCIS and the Department of State.

_____ Also very important are the documents you brought from your native country, such as your passport, birth certificate, marriage certificate, and divorce certificate. Make copies of them and store each set in a different safe place because it will be difficult to replace them. If at all possible, also file high school and college diplomas and proof, such as special school certificates, that show you have special training or skills.

Remember (write in your diary or calendar) where you've placed your material. Sometimes we do such a good job of placing papers in safe places that we can't find them later!

CHAPTER 13

When You Need a Lawyer

TRYING TO GET A GREEN CARD isn't easy. Dealing with government agencies can be frustrating. The language on instructions and forms can be hard to understand. The forms can be hard to fill out. You may have questions, but no one you trust to answer them. And, in procedures that may take many months or years, it's almost impossible to keep up with changes.

This book helps you to make sense out of the process. The websites for the USCIS and the Department of State may give you added information. But the sites are often confusing and unclear. Sometimes, as they admit, they don't even tell you everything you need to know.

Asking an immigration lawyer for advice may be a good idea. After all, this is probably one of the most important times of your life. You want to get it right.

See the USCIS website: Finding Legal Advice.

The Search for a Dependable Lawyer

Finding a lawyer who is honest and careful, who is an expert in immigration, whom you trust, and with whom you feel comfortable may take some work. As Americans like to say, "You have to do your homework."

Your lawyer must be competent, reliable, and willing to be fairly generous with time. Don't be embarrassed about interviewing any lawyer you are thinking of hiring. A good lawyer will help you to make sure that you are a good fit for each other. Here are some ways to find the right immigration lawyer.

Contact the USCIS

The USCIS suggests that you call the district, or field, office near your home for a list of nonprofit organizations that may be able to help you apply for an immigration benefit. Nonprofit groups work for the community, not to make a big profit. But they do charge. And, because they use limited government money to keep them running, they may not be as dependable as a good private lawyer.

Bar Associations

Lawyers' groups are called bar associations. One group that should be dependable and that may refer someone to you is the American Immigration Lawyers Association (www.aila.org).

State Bar Associations

On their state bar websites, California, Florida, North Carolina, and Texas list lawyers who passed tests and now specialize in immigration law. The websites and phone numbers are:

California
Phone: 800-843-9053
members.calbar.ca.gov/

Florida
Phone: 850-561-5600
www.floridabar.org/names.nsf

North Carolina
Phone: 919-828-4620
www.ncbar.com/members/member_directory.asp

Texas
Phone: 512-463-1463
www.texasbar.com

Word of Mouth
Chances are, you have friends and relatives who have used immigration lawyers. Ask them for advice. But be careful. Ask how satisfied they were. Find out how their cases worked out. Dig a little. Don't hire someone just because he or she is a relative or a friend of a friend.

Advertisements
These can be risky. Just because someone advertises, doesn't mean he or she is skillful or honest. If you like the sound of someone in an ad, ask around the community about the lawyer's reputation. Call your local lawyers' group to ask if the lawyer has had any lawsuits filed against him or her.

Keeping Watch
How much does the lawyer charge? Some lawyers charge a big fee to begin with and then hourly rates. These fees can add up quickly. At your first meeting or even before, settle on a rate that is fair to both of you and that you can afford. Ask if the lawyer will charge for every question you ask, which will make you afraid of or uncomfortable about phoning too often and causing charges. Such a lawyer is not the right person for you if you need a lot of time spent on your case.

Is the person a real immigration lawyer? Be careful of anyone who claims to be an expert, but isn't a licensed immigration lawyer. Don't allow someone to give you information that sounds sort of right, but isn't. Many people will say they can help you. The Internet and even some stores in your neighborhood list such so-called specialists.

Remember: No one—no private group and no person—can claim to have a special connection to the USCIS.

Remember: No one can promise to get you the results you want or to get your case rushed through the process.

In many countries, the word *notario* means that someone is a lawyer. This isn't true in the United States. Here, notarios, notary publics, and immigration consultants aren't licensed immigration lawyers. They aren't allowed to give you legal advice. They aren't allowed to answer immigration questions. Only a licensed immigration lawyer can appear before the USCIS on your behalf.

The USCIS has a free booklet, "Don't Be a Victim of Immigration Fraud" in Spanish, Creole, Chinese, Polish, and English. You can get it at http://www.uscis.gov/legaladvice or by calling customer service at 1-800-375-5283.

If You Can't Afford a Lawyer

You can get free or less costly legal help. The Board of Immigration Appeals (BIA) has the names of groups that give immigration help. Some may charge a small fee, far less than most lawyers do, or provide their services free of charge (pro bono). For a list of organizations, go to http://www.usdoj.gov/eoir/statspub/raroster.htm. Look for recognition, accreditation roster.

Qualified representatives provide services pro bono or for little cost. They include law school students or graduates who know immigration law and how to work with cases in court. To make sure the representative is accredited and belongs to a recognized organization, ask to see a copy of the BIA decision that makes him or her official. A representative must file Form G-26, Notice of Entry of Appearance as Attorney or Representative, along with your application or petition. If you are filing your documents overseas, an accredited lawyer from the country you are in may represent you.

The office of the Chief Immigration Judge has a **list of lawyers and groups** that may represent immigrants in court proceedings. However, they may not be able to help you with preparing forms or filing petitions and other routine work that doesn't involve the immigration courts. For the list, go to http://www.usdoj.gov/eoir/probono/states.htm or call the public affairs department at the Department of Justice, 703-305-0289.

Questions to Ask Yourself	Yes	No
Did I make sure there are no court cases against my lawyer?	_____	_____
Am I at ease with my lawyer?	_____	_____
Does my lawyer listen to me?	_____	_____
Does my lawyer take careful notes?	_____	_____
Does my lawyer return phone calls in a timely way?	_____	_____
Is my lawyer organized and efficient?	_____	_____

All your answers should be "yes" or this lawyer may not be right for you.

Questions to Ask Your Lawyer	Lawyer's Answer
1. May I see your license?	_____
2. Have you handled cases like mine?	_____
3. How did they turn out?	_____
4. Exactly what will you charge?	_____
5. Do you accept money orders?	_____
6. Is there a consultation (first meeting) fee?	_____
7. How will you charge?*	_____

_____

*Here are some ways lawyers charge:

➤ by 15-minute time periods (every phone call will cost you)

➤ by the hour (ask for a schedule and an estimate of costs)

➤ flat fee (can you pay in installations?)

8. May I meet my case's paralegal?* _____

9. Will you personally review my forms? _____

10. What should I take to our first meeting? _____

11. When will I receive my contract? _____

Your Responsibilities to Your Lawyer

1. Come prepared to your meetings. Take along copies of all the paperwork you will need.
2. Write down your questions ahead of time.
3. Take along paper and pen for notes.
4. Get to know immigration rules. Understand what the lawyer and paralegal are talking about.
5. Keep track of deadlines and appointments.
6. Always be on time—whether at the law office or at the USCIS or in court.

---

*What is a paralegal?

Most good lawyers are very busy. They don't want to spend their time or your money sitting down with you and filling out forms or answering simple questions. Or they may not be fluent in your language. So, many lawyers will turn you over to a trained assistant, who isn't a lawyer but has law training and may speak the same language you do, besides English. It's possible that you will spend more time with the paralegal than with the lawyer. Being comfortable with this person is also important. Take notes and keep copies of all dealings you have with the paralegal, just as with the lawyer.

Protect Yourself! Watch Out for Fraud!

It cannot be said enough: There are people who will try to cheat you.

Here is a warning from the U.S. Department of State: "Some consultants, travel agencies, real estate offices, and people called 'notaries public' offer immigration services. Be sure to **ask questions about their qualifications.** Ask to **see copies of their Board of Immigration Appeals (BIA) accreditation letter or bar certificate.** Some people who say they are qualified to offer legal services are not qualified. These people can make mistakes that cause serious problems for you. If you use an immigration consultant or lawyer, always **get a written contract.** The contract should be in English and in your own language, if English is not your native language. The contract should list all services that will be provided to you and how much they cost. **Ask for references** before you sign the contract.

If possible, **don't pay cash** for services. Get a receipt for your payments. Be sure to keep your original documents. **Never sign a blank form** or application. **Understand what you are signing.**

If you believe you have been cheated, call your state or local district attorney, city consumer affairs department, or local police department. Your local phone book will have their numbers on special pages (at the front of most books) that list official phone numbers."

Don't be afraid to call. If you don't report someone who cheats you, that person will go on to cheat others.

CHAPTER 14

The Light at the End of the Tunnel

AT LAST IT'S TIME for your final steps to getting a green card. You will be changing your status from nonimmigrant (with an approved visa petition or a lottery win) to permanent resident. You have a choice of two paths to take. One is consular processing (CP). The other is adjustment of status (AOS). Some immigration lawyers believe that because of the weak economy, especially the loss of jobs, and changes in laws, it may be better to use AOS. But, really, it depends on your situation.

Adjustment of status is available only in the United States, which means, of course, that you need to be here. CP, which can be a shorter process, requires applicants to be interviewed at an overseas U.S. consulate. But that may be complicated by local problems.

If you decide to use adjustment of status, you must file forms with the USCIS and be interviewed at your local agency office. That seems convenient. But you may not be allowed to stay in the United States while you're waiting for your green card. If you can answer "yes" to each of the following questions, then adjustment of status may be the right path for you.

	Yes	No
1. Are you the immediate relative of a U.S. citizen?	____	____
2. Are you here legally?	____	____
3. Have you been legal ever since arriving here?	____	____
4. Have you stayed within your visa dates?	____	____
5. Can you make use of the old 245(i) law?	____	____
6. Have you always worked with a legal work permit?	____	____

You may need an immigration lawyer if you spent more than 180 days in the United States illegally or you are not sure of your answers to these six questions.

If you are sure that you are eligible for adjustment of status, here are examples of forms to fill out and some documents you need to give the USCIS.

◆ proof that you are eligible for a green card, such as an approved **Form I-130**
◆ letter from the DOS saying that you've won the lottery
◆ copies of your fiancé(e) visa petition approval, the **Form I-94** card, and your marriage certificate
◆ proof that you're an immediate relative
◆ **Form I-485**, Application to Register Permanent Resident or Adjust Status
◆ **Form G-325A**, Biographic Information
◆ **Form I-864**, Affidavit of Support and documents to support this
◆ letter from employer including dates of employment, salary, and job description
◆ **Form I-693**, medical examination
◆ if immigrating through registry, proof that you've been in the United States since January 1972

◆ two passport-style color photos of yourself
◆ filing fee

Get Ready for Your Interview

You may have an interview with the USCIS before you finally receive your green card. The USCIS will send you a letter giving you the date of the interview and where it will be held and what you should take along. (Not every applicant has an interview.) Most interviews last less than half an hour.

Some suggestions for your interview:

_____ Dress in an appropriate way.

_____ Make copies of all papers you'll give or show to the USCIS.

_____ Take the strongest proof you have to prove such events as marriage.

_____ Take an interpreter if you don't speak English well.

_____ Know exactly where you have to go. Work out how you'll get there.

_____ Be on time. Leave yourself time to walk or park and to go through security.

_____ Make your answers short. Be honest. Be clear. Don't chat.

_____ Relax.

That's it. After you're approved, watch for your green card in the mail. It will be sent in several weeks or months. But it will come. You are now a permanent resident. Welcome!

If you are overseas and will use consular processing, it means you have been through the necessary steps and are eligible for a green card. Go to your nearest U.S. embassy or consulate to complete your application. If you are abroad, don't try to enter the United States to finish your visa procedure. That will lead to serious problems. You've come too far for that to happen.

The National Visa Center (NVC), a central office in the United States, will send you **Form DS-3032,** Choice of Address and Agent. If you're not using a lawyer, the agent is the person who will receive your immigration mail. You will have to return Form DS-3032 with the visa processing fee and a security surcharge. You must pay by money order, not by personal check, and make it out to the Department of State. At about the same time, your sponsor will receive a bill for Form I-864, Affidavit of Support, and must pay the fee.

The NVC will transfer your file to your nearest embassy and will send you more forms. You'll be told where to send them. You will have to send originals, so remember to include a copy of every document and keep a second copy for your files. The originals will eventually be returned to you. You may hear from the embassy directly instead of the NVC. Whomever you hear from, carefully follow the instructions. You don't want your package returned because you have to make corrections.

Here are the forms and documents you'll have to deal with. (When you're ready to send them, check off each on the list.)

_____ **Form DS-2001,** Notification of Applicant(s) Readiness

_____ **Form DS-230 Part I,** Application for Immigrant Visa and Alien Registration

_____ information pages of current passports for every family member immigrating

_____ birth certificates for you and your family, with English translations

_____ police certificate for everyone over 16 years old, from every country in which each of you lived for more than six months

_____ marriage, death, divorce certificates or annulment decree showing your marital status and history

_____ military record and discharge papers, if appropriate

_____ court and prison records if appropriate

_____ proof of your assets, such as real estate deeds, bank accounts, anything that shows you have assets and won't end up being a public charge

_____ letter from your sponsor's employer with his or her work history and salary and a description of the job

_____ **Form DS-230 Part II**, Application for Immigrant Visa and Alien Registration. Each applicant must submit one and sign it before a U.S. consular officer after your interview

_____ **Form I-864** or Form I-864EZ, Affidavit of Support and short form

_____ financial documents in support of Form I-864, such as bank statements, tax returns, and the job letter

Get Ready for Your Interview

Before your interview, you will be fingerprinted and have a background check done. You will also have to set aside time for your medical exam by a doctor who is approved by the consulate. (There is probably a list.)

Then you will receive a notice of the date, time, and location of your interview. It will take about half an hour. The person sponsoring you doesn't have to attend but it wouldn't hurt if he or she does. This is especially true if you are immigrating on the basis of marriage. The consular official will probably ask many detailed questions about how you and your spouse met, your courtship, your wedding, and your marriage. Be prepared.

For your interview, you will need:

_____ four color, passport-style photographs

_____ up-to-date passports for your family

_____ medical exam and vaccination reports

_____ income tax forms for the time you worked in the United States

_____ unpaid visa fees (money orders only for the exact amount)

Some suggestions for your interview:

_____ Dress in an appropriate way.

_____ Make copies of all papers you'll leave or show.

_____ Take the strongest proof you have to prove such events as marriage.

_____ Ask for an interpreter if you don't speak English well.

_____ Know exactly where you have to go. Figure out how you'll get there and how long it will take.

_____ Be on time. Leave yourself more than enough time to walk or park and to go through security.

_____ Make your answers to questions short. Be honest. Be clear. Don't chat.

_____ Relax.

What Happens Next?

You have to wait just a little while longer. The end is in sight. Depending on what still needs to be done with your process, it may take up to four months for the embassy to let you know that you've been approved for an immigrant visa.

Your visa will be good for six months. (It is possible, but not advisable, to ask for an extension.) The embassy will give you the Immigrant Visa and Alien Registration with your photo and an approval stamp. Your original DS-230, your personal documents, and the X-rays from your medical exam will be returned to you. You will need to give them to immigration officers when you arrive in the United States.

When you go through the immigration line in the airport, ship terminal, or border crossing, an officer will take and keep all your papers except your X-rays. The papers will go into your file. The officer will stamp your passport to show you are a lawful permanent resident. Your **Form I-94**, Record of Arrival and Departure, will be stamped with an employment authorization that is good for six months.

In time, your green card will arrive in the mail. Your long wait is over. You are now a permanent resident. Welcome!

Where's My Card?

If you've been given permanent resident status and 60 days have passed but your green card hasn't come, call 800-375-5283.

Who and Where to Call

IF YOU DON'T KNOW which department to call, use this general information number: 800-333-4636.

Department of Homeland Security (DHS)
U.S. Department of Homeland Security
Washington, DC 20528
http://www.dhs.gov

U.S. Citizenship and Immigration Services (USCIS)
Phone, customer service: 800-375-5283
For hearing impaired: 800-767-1833
http://www.uscis.gov

For USCIS forms, call 800-870-3676 or look on the USCIS website.

U.S. Customs and Border Protection (CBP)
Phone: 202-354-1000
http://www.cbp.gov

U.S. Immigration and Customs Enforcement (ICE)
http://www.ice.gov

U.S. Department of State (DOS)
2201 C Street NW
Washington, DC 20520
Phone: 202-647-4000
http://www.state.gov

U.S. Department of State
Intercountry Adoption
U.S. Department of State
Office of Children's Issues
SA-29
2201 C Street NW
Washington, DC 20520
E-mail: AskCI@state.gov (general
  questions)
  AdoptionUSCA@state.gov (Hague
  Adoption Convention questions)
Phone: 888-407-4747 (from the United
  States or Canada)
202-501-4444 (outside the United
  States or Canada)
Fax: 202-736-9080

**Important Information for New
  Immigrants**
http://www.welcometousa.gov

Public Libraries

Some libraries give free classes on how to use the Internet. Some libraries and schools, such as community (two-year) colleges also give free or low-cost English language classes and have other programs for children and adults.

Postal Codes

You will see two-letter abbreviations in most addresses. These are used by the post office instead of writing out state or territory names.

AL	Alabama	**FL**	Florida
AK	Alaska	**GA**	Georgia
AZ	Arizona	**HI**	Hawaii
AR	Arkansas	**ID**	Idaho
CA	California	**IL**	Illinois
CO	Colorado	**IN**	Indiana
CT	Connecticut	**IA**	Iowa
DC	Washington, DC	**KS**	Kansas
DE	Delaware	**KY**	Kentucky

LA	Louisiana	**OK**	Oklahoma
ME	Maine	**OR**	Oregon
MD	Maryland	**PA**	Pennsylvania
MA	Massachusetts	**RI**	Rhode Island
MI	Michigan	**SC**	South Carolina
MN	Minnesota	**SD**	South Dakota
MS	Mississippi	**TN**	Tennessee
MO	Missouri	**TX**	Texas
MT	Montana	**UT**	Utah
NE	Nebraska	**VT**	Vermont
NV	Nevada	**VA**	Virginia
NH	New Hampshire	**WA**	Washington
NJ	New Jersey	**WV**	West Virginia
NM	New Mexico	**WI**	Wisconsin
NY	New York	**WY**	Wyoming
NC	North Carolina	**PR**	Puerto Rico
ND	North Dakota	**VI**	Virgin Islands
OH	Ohio		

USCIS Local Offices

To speak in person to someone at the USCIS, you will have to visit a local office. Not all these offices are really local; some are in neighboring states. But, in the past, going to the USCIS could take hours. Now you can make an appointment and, as long as you show up on time, things will go smoothly and quickly.

In-person visits are mainly for people who have problems with filed applications and petitions that could not be taken care of in a phone call. For other problems, the USCIS suggests that, before going to an office, you first use its website or call customer service. Customer service should be able to help you check information, get help, get forms, and find out if anything has changed with the process or with forms since you filled them out. Most forms need to be mailed. Some applications can be sent by computer. A few forms may be given directly to your local office.

The toll-free USCIS phone number is 800-375-5283. The TTY number is 800-767-1833.

To visit an office or to speak with an immigration information officer, you must schedule your appointment with the USCIS. Or you can go to InfoPass on the USCIS website, which gives information in 12 languages. As you can see from the list of offices that follows, some offices have special days set aside for people with InfoPass appointments. **Important:** You must bring the printout of your InfoPass appointment and a photo ID with you. The website is http://infopass.uscis.gov

The USCIS Service and Office Locator site is very helpful. All you need is your zip code to find out where your office is. This is important if your state has more than one office. Each office listing gives exact transportation directions and information about filing at egov.uscis.gov/crisgwi.

Calling on the Phone

The USCIS is trying to make its services run better. But it still is a government bureaucracy. That means not everyone who works there will be friendly and helpful. Here are some hints about calling.

➤ Keep your receipt and priority numbers and any other identification you may need close to the phone.

➤ Gather the notes or paperwork you have questions about before you dial.

➤ Think about what you want to ask. You could write down a little speech or notes with the points you wish to make.

➤ Listen carefully to any recorded messages or you will have to go through the entire dialing process again.

➤ If you think you got the wrong answer, call to speak to a different person. If you reach someone who is unhelpful, say "thank you," hang up, wait a little while, and try again. Ask for a supervisor if you feel you cannot get the right information no matter how many times you call.

➤ Be patient. Never lose your temper. It won't help. You don't want to anger people who are supposed to help you.

Location of Local Offices

ALABAMA
Atlanta Field Office
2150 Parklake Drive
Atlanta, GA 30345

ALASKA
Anchorage Field Office
620 East 10th Avenue, Suite 102
Anchorage, AK 99501
The Anchorage Field Office still accepts
a limited number of walk-ins—people
without appointments—on a first come,
first serve basis. Please note that walk-
ins may have to wait to see an immigration information officer, since those with
an INFOPASS will be seen first.

ARIZONA
Phoenix Field Office
2035 North Central Avenue
Phoenix, AZ 85004
This office serves the following counties:
Apache, Coconino, Gila, Greenlee, La
Paz, Maricopa, Mohave, Navajo,
Yavapai, and Yuma.

Tucson Field Office
6431 South Country Club Road
Tucson, AZ 85706
This office serves Pima, Santa Cruz,
Cochise, Graham, and Pinal counties.

ARKANSAS
Fort Smith Field Office
4977 Old Greenwood Road
Fort Smith, AR 7290
This office serves these counties: Ashley,
Baxter, Benton, Boone, Bradley,
Calhoun, Carroll, Clark, Columbia,
Crawford, Franklin, Garland,
Hempstead, Hot Spring, Howard,
Johnson, Lafayette, Little River, Logan,
Madison, Marion, Miller, Montgomery,
Nevada, Newton, Ouachita, Pike, Polk,
Scott, Searcy, Sebastian, Sevier, Union,
and Washington.

Memphis Field Office
842 Virginia Run Cove
Memphis, TN 38122
The office hours are Monday through
Thursday from 7:30 A.M. until 2 P.M. and
Friday from 7:30 A.M. until 1:00 P.M.
This office serves the state of Tennessee
and also serves the following counties
in Arkansas: Arkansas, Chloot, Clay,
Cleburne, Cleveland, Conway,
Craighead, Crittenden, Cross, Dallas,
Desha, Drew, Faulkner, Fulton, Grant,
Greene, Independence, Izard, Jackson,
Jefferson, Lawrence, Lee, Lincoln,
Lonoke, Mississippi, Monroe, Perry,
Phillips, Poinsett, Pope, Prairie, Pulaski,
Randolph, Saint Francis, Saline, Sharp,
Stone, Van Buren, White, Woodruff,
and Yell.
Also see the entry for this office in
Mississippi to see what counties this
office serves in that state.

CALIFORNIA
Chula Vista Field Office
1261 3rd Avenue, Suite A
Chula Vista, CA 91911

San Diego Field Office
880 Front Street
San Diego, CA 92101
The Chula Vista and San Diego Field
Offices are closed on Wednesdays.
Residents of San Diego county may
schedule an InfoPass appointment at
either the San Diego or Chula Vista
Field Office. The San Diego Field Office
only provides a limited number of time
slots for InfoPass appointments.

Fresno Field Office
1177 Fulton Mall
Fresno, CA 93721
This office is closed the first Friday of
every month.
This office serves Fresno, Inyo, Kern,
Kings, Madera, Mariposa, Merced,
Mono, Stanislaus, and Tulare counties.

Imperial Field Office
509 Industry Way
Imperial, CA 92251
The information window is closed on
Wednesdays.

Los Angeles Field Office
300 North Los Angeles Street
Los Angeles, CA 90012
This office serves the counties of Los
Angeles, Santa Barbara, San Luis
Obispo, and Ventura.

Sacramento Field Office
650 Capitol Mall
Sacramento, CA 95814
No cameras or camera phones may be
used in this office. Do not bring these
items with you as you may be kept out
of the building.

San Bernardino Field Office
655 West Rialto Avenue
San Bernardino, CA 92410
This office serves the counties of San
Bernardino and Riverside.

San Diego Field Office
880 Front Street
San Diego, CA 92101.

San Francisco Field Office
444 Washington Street
San Francisco, CA 94111
Mailing Address
USCIS
630 Sansome Street
San Francisco, CA 94111
This office serves the following counties:
Alameda, Contra Costa, Del Norte,
Humboldt, Lake, Marin, Mendocino,
Napa, San Francisco, San Mateo,
Sonoma, and Trinity.

San Jose Field Office
1887 Monterey Road
San Jose, CA 95112
Visitors are not allowed to use cameras
or camera phones in this office. Don't
bring these items with you or you may
be kept out of the building.
This office serves Santa Clara, Santa
Cruz, San Benito, and Monterey
counties.

Santa Ana Field Office
34 Civic Center Plaza
Santa Ana, CA 92701
Mailing Address
34 Civic Center Plaza, 1st Floor, Mail
Room
Santa Ana, CA 92701
Cell phones with cameras or any other
recording devices are not allowed in
the Santa Ana Office.

This office mainly serves Orange County. It also serves Los Angeles, Ventura, Santa Barbara, and San Luis Obispo counties.

COLORADO
Denver Field Office
4730 Paris Street
Denver, CO 80239

CONNECTICUT
Hartford Field Office
450 Main Street, 1st Floor
Hartford, CT 06103
This office is closed to the public on the third Friday of every month.

DELAWARE
Dover Field Office
655 South Bay Road, Suite 4E
Dover, DE 19901

DISTRICT OF COLUMBIA
(Washington, DC
Washington Field Office
2675 Prosperity Avenue
Fairfax, VA 22031
The Information Unit closes every Thursday at 11:00 A.M. INFOPASS appointments are not available during these afternoon hours. The office is closed on the first Thursday of each month and on all federal holidays.
This office serves the State of Virginia and the District of Columbia.

Special notes from the Washington, DC, office

Request to reschedule an interview:
If you want to reschedule or postpone your interview, you must send a written request to was.interviewreschedule @dhs.gov. Your request must be received before the scheduled interview date and include your alien number, which is written on the appointment notice. Your request must also include the reason(s) for the request to reschedule; you must be very specific when giving your reason(s).
A Washington field office employee will let you know if your request is granted. The Washington field office will only reschedule an interview if there are strong reasons you cannot control that make it impossible for you to attend the interview.

Request a sign language interpreter:
If you are scheduled for an interview or an oath ceremony and you require a sign language interpreter, the Washington field office can provide one for you. Write to was.accommodatlon@dhs.gov and give your name, your alien number (which appears on your appointment notice), your appointment date, and your appointment time. The office will contact you about the arrangements that can be made.

Bringing small children to an interview:
Unless the presence of your child is needed at an interview, do not take along small children. There may be no place for them to wait.

FLORIDA
Hialeah Field Office
5880 NW 183rd Street
Hialeah, Florida 33015
This office mainly serves the eastern portion of Broward county and the northern portion of Miami-Dade county.

Jacksonville Field Office
4121 Southpoint Boulevard
Jacksonville, FL 32216
This office serves these counties:
Alachua, Baker, Bay, Bradford,
Calhoun, Clay, Columbia, Dixie, Duval,
Escambia, Franklin, Gadsden, Gilchrist,
Gulf, Hamilton, Holmes, Jackson,
Jefferson, Lafayette, Leon, Levy, Liberty,
Madison, Nassau, Okaloosa, Putnam,
Santa Rosa, St. Johns, Suwanee,
Taylor, Union, Wakulla, Walton, and
Washington.
This office also serves Flagler and
Volusia counties for Form I-485
(Application for Lawful Permanent
Residence) applicants. This includes
anything to do with specific cases,
such as emergency advance parole,
interim employment authorization docu-
ments, InfoPass inquiries, and requests
for information.

Kendall Field Office
14675 SW 120th Street
Miami, FL 33186
This office primarily serves the southern
portion of Collier county, Monroe county,
and the southern portion of Miami-Dade.

Miami Field Office
8801 NW 7th Avenue
Miami, FL 33150
This office serves the northeastern portion of Miami-Dade county.

Orlando Field Office
6680 Corporate Centre Boulevard
Orlando, FL 32822
This office serves Orange, Osceola,
Seminole, Lake, Brevard, Flagler,
Volusia, Marion, and Sumter counties.

Tampa Field Office
5524 West Cypress Street
Tampa, FL 33607
This office serves Citrus, Charlotte,
Desoto, Hardee, Hernando,
Hillsborough, Lee, Manatee, Pasco,
Pinellas, Polk, and Sarasota counties.

West Palm Beach Field Office
920 Banyan Boulevard
West Palm Beach, FL 33401
This office serves Glades, Hendry,
Highlands, Indian River, Martin,
Okeechobee, Palm Beach and St.
Lucie counties.

GEORGIA
Atlanta Field Office
2150 Parklake Drive
Atlanta, Georgia 30345

GUAM
Agana Field Office
Sirena Plaza, Suite 100
108 Hernan Cortez Avenue
Hagatna, Guam 96910

HAWAII
Honolulu Field Office
595 Ala Moana Boulevard
Honolulu, Hawaii 96813
Fingerprints are only taken at the
Honolulu Application Support Center,
677 Ala Moana Boulevard, Suite 102,
Honolulu, Hawaii 96813-5417. For
more information on this office, go to
the Application Support Center section of the USCIS Office Locator.

IDAHO
Boise Field Office
1185 South Vinnell Way
Boise, ID 83709
This office is closed on Wednesdays
from 12:00 P.M. until 4 P.M.
This office serves the counties of: Ada,
Adams, Bannock, Bear Lake, Bingham,
Blaine, Boise, Bonneville, Butte, Camas,
Canyon, Caribou, Cassia, Clark, Custer,
Elmore, Franklin, Fremont, Gem,
Gooding, Jefferson, Jerome, Lemhi,
Lincoln, Madison, Minidoka, Oneida,
Owyhee, Payette, Power, Teton, Twin
Falls, Valley, and Washington.

Spokane Field Office
U.S. Courthouse
920 West Riverside, Room 691
Spokane, WA 99201
This office is closed on Fridays.
You must bring a photo ID when visiting
this office. If you are unable to sched-
ule an appointment using InfoPass, you
may send an appointment request by
mail to USCIS, U.S. Courthouse, 920
West Riverside, Spokane, WA 99201.
In addition to serving 12 counties in
Washington, this office also serves the
following counties in Idaho: Benewah,
Bonner, Boundary, Clearwater, Idaho,
Kootenai, Latah, Lewis, Nez Perce, and
Shoshone.

ILLINOIS
Chicago Field Office
101 West Congress Parkway
Chicago, IL 60605
This office provides immigration benefits
to applicants residing in the states of
Illinois and Wisconsin and the follow-
ing counties in Northwest Indiana:
Lake, Porter, LaPorte, and Saint
Joseph.

St. Louis Field Office
Robert A. Young Federal Building
1222 Spruce Street
St. Louis, MO 63103-2815
In addition to serving over 50 counties in
Missouri, this office serves the follow-
ing counties in Illinois: Alexander,
Bond, Calhoun, Clark, Clay, Clinton,
Crawford, Cumberland, Edwards,
Effingham, Fayette, Franklin, Gallatin,
Hamilton, Hardin, Jackson, Jasper,
Jefferson, Jersey, Johnson, Lawrence,
Madison, Marion, Massac, Monroe,
Perry, Pope, Pulaski, Randolph,
Richland, Saint Clair, Saline, Union,
Wabash, Washington, Wayne, White,
and Williamson.

INDIANA
Chicago Field Office
101 West Congress Parkway
Chicago, IL 60605
This office provides immigration benefits
to applicants residing in the states of
Illinois and Wisconsin and the follow-
ing counties in Northwest Indiana:
Lake, Porter, LaPorte, and Saint
Joseph.

Indianapolis Field Office
Gateway Plaza Building
950 North Meridian Street, Room 400
Indianapolis, IN 46204
This office serves Indiana, except for
those served by the Chicago district
office.

IOWA
Des Moines Field Office
210 Walnut Street, Room 369
Federal Building
Des Moines, IA 50309
The Des Moines Field Office is closed to
the public on Wednesdays.

The Des Moines Field Office serves the following counties: Adair, Adams, Allamakee, Appanoose, Benton, Blackhawk, Boone, Bremer, Buchanan, Butler, Calhoun, Cedar, Cerro Gordo, Chickasaw, Clarke, Clayton, Clinton, Dallas, Davis, Decatur, Delaware, Des Moines, Dubuque, Fayette, Floyd, Franklin, Grundy, Guthrie, Hamilton, Hancock, Hardin, Henry, Howard, Humboldt, Iowa, Jackson, Jasper, Jefferson, Johnson, Jones, Keokuk, Kossuth, Lee, Linn, Louisa, Lucas, Madison, Mahaska, Marion, Marshall, Mitchell, Monroe, Muscatine, Polk, Poweshiek, Ringgold, Scott, Story, Tama, Union, Van Buren, Wapello, Warren, Washington, Wayne, Webster, Winnebago, Winneshiek, Worth, and Wright.

Omaha Field Office

1717 Avenue H
Omaha, NE 68110
Please call (402) 633-4056 to check on a change in the hours of operations or the closing of the Omaha Field Office during bad weather or other conditions.
NOTE: This office is closed for InfoPass appointments on Wednesdays.
In addition to more than 90 counties in Nebraska, the Omaha Field Office serves the following counties in Iowa: Audubon, Buena Vista, Carroll, Cass, Cherokee, Clay, Crawford, Dickinson, Emmet, Fremont, Greene, Harrison, Ida, Mills, Monona, Montgomery, O'Brien, Osceola, Page, Palo Alto, Plymouth, Pocahontas, Pottawattamie, Sac, Shelby, Sioux, Taylor, and Woodbury.

KANSAS
Kansas City Field Office

9747 NW Conant Avenue
Kansas City, MO 64153

In addition to serving over 60 counties in Missouri, this office serves the following counties in Kansas: Allen, Anderson, Atchison, Bourbon, Brown, Coffey, Doniphan, Douglas, Franklin, Geary, Jackson, Jefferson, Johnson, Leavenworth, Linn, Lyon, Marshall, Miami, Morris, Nemaha, Osage, Pottawatomie, Riley, Shawnee, Wabaunsee, Washington, Woodson, and Wyandotte.

Wichita Field Office

271 West 3rd Street North, Suite 1050
Wichita, KS 67202
These offices are closed for InfoPass appointment on Wednesdays.
This office serves the following counties in Kansas: Barber, Barton, Butler, Chase, Chautauqua, Cherokee, Cheyenne, Clark, Clay, Cloud, Comanche, Cowley, Crawford, Decatur, Dickinson, Edwards, Elk, Ellis, Ellsworth, Finney, Ford, Gove, Graham, Grant, Gray, Greeley, Greenwood, Hamilton, Harper, Harvey, Haskell, Hodgeman, Jewell, Kearny, Kingman, Kiowa, Labette, Lane, Lincoln, Logan, Marion, McPherson, Mead, Mitchell, Montgomery, Morton, Neosho, Ness, Norton, Osborne, Ottawa, Pawnee, Phillips, Pratt, Rawlins, Republic, Rice, Reno, Rooks, Rush, Russell, Saline, Scott, Sedgwick, Seward, Sheridan, Sherman, Smith, Stafford, Stanton, Stevens, Sumner, Thomas, Trego, Wallace, Wichita, and Wilson.

KENTUCKY
Louisville Field Office
Gene Snyder U.S. Courthouse and
 Custom House
601 West Broadway, Suite 390
Louisville, KY 40202
This office is closed on Wednesdays.

LOUISIANA
New Orleans Field Office
Metairie Centre, Suite 300 (Third Floor)
2424 Edenborn Avenue
Metairie, LA 70001
This office is closed on Fridays.

MAINE
Portland Field Office
176 Gannett Drive South
Portland, Maine 04106

MARYLAND
Baltimore Field Office
Fallon Federal Building
31 Hopkins Plaza, First Floor
Baltimore, MD 21201

MASSACHUSETTS
Boston Field Office
John F. Kennedy Federal Building
Government Center, Room E-160
Boston, MA 02203

MICHIGAN
Detroit Field Office
333 Mount Elliott
Detroit, MI 48207
The Information Unit for InfoPass
 appointments is located at:
260 Mount Elliott
Detroit, MI 48207
This office is closed the first Wednesday
 of each month.

MINNESOTA
Saint Paul Field Office
2901 Metro Drive, Suite 100
Bloomington, MN 55425
In addition to serving the state of
 Minnesota, this also serves the states
 of North Dakota and South Dakota, as
 well as over 30 counties in Wisconsin.

MISSISSIPPI
Jackson Satellite Office
100 West Capitol Street, Suite 727
Jackson MS 39269
This office serves Bolivar, Calhoun,
 Carroll, Chickasaw, Choctaw, Clay,
 George, Hancock, Harrison, Hinds,
 Humphreys, Jackson, Leake, Leflore,
 Lowndes, Madison, Monroe,
 Montgomery, Neshoba, Oktibbeha,
 Pearl, Rankin, Scott, Stone, Sunflower,
 Tallahatchie, Washington, Webster,
 Yalobusha, and Yazoo counties.
The office hours are: Monday through
 Friday from 8:00 A.M. until 3:30 P.M.

Memphis Field Office
842 Virginia Run Cove
Memphis, TN 38122
The office hours are Monday through
 Thursday from 7:30 A.M. until 2:00 P.M.
 and Friday from 7:30 A.M. until 1:00 P.M.
In addition to serving the state of
 Tennessee and over 40 counties in
 Arkansas, this office serves the follow-
 ing counties in Mississippi: Alcorn,
 Attala, Benton, Bolivar, Calhoun,
 Carrol, Chickasaw, Choctaw, Clay,
 Coahoma, Desoto, Grenada,
 Humphreys, Itawamba, Lafayette, Lee,
 Leflore, Lowndes, Marshall, Monroe,
 Montgomery, Panola, Pontotoc,
 Prentiss, Quitman, Sunflower,
 Tallahatchie, Tate, Tippah, Tishomingo,
 Tunica, Union, Washington, Webster,
 Winston, and Yalobusha.

New Orleans Field Office
Metairie Centre, Suite 300 (third floor)
2424 Edenborn Avenue
Metairie, LA 70001
This office is closed on Fridays.
This office serves the state of Louisiana
and the southern half of Mississippi,
comprising the counties of: Adams,
Amite, Claiborne, Clarke, Copiah,
Covington, Forrest, Franklin, George,
Greene, Hancock, Harrison, Hinds,
Holmes, Issaquena, Jackson, Jasper,
Jefferson, Jones, Kemper, Lamar,
Lauderdale, Lawrence, Leake, Lincoln,
Madison, Marion, Neshoba, Newton,
Noxubee, Pearl River, Perry, Pike,
Rankin, Scott, Sharkey, Simpson,
Smith, Stone, Walthall, Warren,
Wayne, Wilkinson, and Yazoo.
If you reside in Louisiana north of the
county of Alexandria or in the counties
listed for Mississippi that are north of
Hattiesburg, you may prefer to visit the
Jackson office for information services.
See the previous entry for address and
information.

MISSOURI
Kansas City Field Office
9747 NW Conant Avenue
Kansas City, MO 64153
This office is closed for InfoPass
appointments on Wednesdays.
This office serves the following counties
in Missouri: Andrew, Atchison, Barry,
Barton, Bates, Benton, Boone,
Buchanan, Caldwell, Callaway,
Camden, Carroll, Cass, Cedar,
Christian, Clay, Clinton, Cole, Cooper,
Dade, Dallas, Daviess, Dekalb,
Douglas, Gentry, Greene, Grundy,
Harrison, Henry, Hickory, Holt,
Howard, Howell, Jackson, Jasper,
Johnson, Laclede, Lafayette,
Lawrence, Livingstone, McDonald,
Mercer, Miller, Moniteau, Morgan,
Newton, Nodaway, Oregon, Osage,
Ozark, Pettis, Platte, Polk, Pulaski,
Putnam, Ray, Saint Clair, Saline,
Stone, Sullivan, Taney, Texas, Vernon,
Webster, Worth, and Wright.
In addition, this office serves 28 coun-
ties in Kansas. See the Kansas entry
for this office for the list of those
counties.

St. Louis Field Office
Robert A. Young Federal Building
1222 Spruce Street
St. Louis, MO 63103-2815
This office serves the following coun-
ties in Missouri: Adair, Audrain,
Bollinger, Butler, Cape Girardeau,
Carter, Chariton, City of Saint Louis,
Clark, Crawford, Dent, Dunklin,
Franklin, Gasconade, Iron, Jefferson,
Knox, Lewis, Lincoln, Linn, Macon,
Madison, Maries, Marion, Mississippi,
Monroe, Montgomery, New Madrid,
Pemiscot, Perry, Phelps, Pike, Ralls,
Randolph, Reynolds, Ripley, Saint
Charles, Saint Francois, Saint
Genevieve, Saint Louis, Schuyler,
Scotland, Scott, Shannon, Shelby,
Stoddard, Warren, Washington, and
Wayne.
In addition, this office also serves almost
40 counties in Illinois. See the entry for
this office in that state for the list of
those counties.

MONTANA
Helena Field Office
2800 Skyway Drive
Helena, MT 59602
This office is closed on Wednesdays.

NEBRASKA
Omaha Field Office
1717 Avenue H
Omaha, NE 68110
Please call 402-633-4056 to check on a
change in the hours of operations or
the closing of the Omaha field office
during bad weather or other conditions.
This office is closed for InfoPass
appointments on Wednesdays.

NEVADA
Las Vegas Field Office
3373 Pepper Lane
Las Vegas, NV 89120
This office serves the following counties
in Nevada: Clark, Esmerelda, Nye, and
Lincoln.

Reno Field Office
1351 Corporate Boulevard
Reno, NV 89502
This office serves the following counties
in Nevada: Carson, Churchill, Douglas,
Elko, Eureka, Humboldt, Lander, Lyon,
Mineral, Pershing, Storey, Washoe, and
White Pine.

NEW HAMPSHIRE
Manchester Field Office
803 Canal Street
Manchester, NH 03101

NEW JERSEY
Mount Laurel Field Office
530 Fellowship Road
Mount Laurel, NJ 08054
This office serves Atlantic, Burlington,
Camden, Cape May, Cumberland,
Gloucester, Mercer, Monmouth,
Ocean, and Salem counties.

Newark Field Office
Peter Rodino Federal Building
970 Broad Street
Newark, NJ 07102
This office serves the counties of
Bergen, Essex, Hudson, Hunterdon,
Middlesex, Morris, Passaic, Somerset,
Sussex, Union, and Warren.

NEW MEXICO
Albuquerque Field Office
1720 Randolph Road
Southeast
Albuquerque, NM 87106
This office is closed for InfoPass
appointments on Wednesdays.
This office serves the following
counties in New Mexico: Bernalillo,
Catron, Cibola, Colfax, Curry,
De Baca, Guadalupe, Harding,
Los Alamos, McKinley, Mora, Quay,
Rio Arriba, Roosevelt, San Juan,
San Miguel, Sandoval, Santa Fe,
Socorro, Taos, Torrence, Valencia,
and Union.

NEW YORK
Albany Field Office
1086 Troy-Schenectady Road
Latham, NY 12110
This office serves the following
counties: Albany, Broome, Chenango,
Clinton, Columbia, Delaware, Essex,
Franklin, Fulton, Greene, Hamilton,
Herkimer, Madison, Montgomery,
Oneida, Otsego, Rensselaer, Saint
Lawrence, Saratoga, Schenectady,
Schoharie, Tioga, Warren, and
Washington.

Buffalo Field Office
Federal Center
130 Delaware Avenue, First Floor
Buffalo, NY 14202
This office serves Alleghany, Cattaraugus,
Cayuga, Chautauqua, Chemung,
Cortland, Erie, Genesee, Jefferson,
Lewis, Livingston, Monroe, Niagara,
Onondaga, Ontario, Orleans, Oswego,
Schuyler, Seneca, Steuben, Tompkins,
Wayne, Wyoming, and Yates counties.

Garden City Field Office
711 Stewart Avenue
Garden City, NY 11530
This office serves Kings, Nassau,
Queens, and Suffolk counties.

New York City Field Office
Jacob Javits Federal Building
26 Federal Plaza, 3rd Floor, Room 3-310
New York, NY 10278
This office serves: Bronx, Kings, Nassau,
New York, Orange, Putnam, Queens,
Richmond, Rockland, Staten Island,
Suffolk, Sullivan, Ulster, and
Westchester counties.

Rochester Field Office
100 State Street, Room 418
Rochester, NY 14614
This office provides limited information
services.

Syracuse Field Office
412 South Warren Street
Syracuse, NY 13202
This office provides limited information
services. The Information Office is
closed on Mondays, Tuesdays, and
Fridays.
This office primarily serves the following
counties: Cayuga, Cortland, Jefferson,
Lewis, Onondaga, Oswego, and
Tompkins.

This satellite office also serves the fol-
lowing counties that lie within the juris-
diction of the Buffalo District Office:
Alleghany, Cattaraugus, Chautauqua,
Chemung, Erie, Genesee, Lewis,
Livingston, Monroe, Niagara, Ontario,
Orleans, Schuyler, Seneca, Steuben,
Wayne, Wyoming, and Yates.

NORTH CAROLINA
Charlotte Field Office
6130 Tyvola Centre Drive
Charlotte, NC 28217
This office is closed for InfoPass
appointments on Fridays.
This office serves Alexander, Alleghany,
Anson, Ashe, Avery, Buncombe, Burke,
Cabarrus, Caldwell, Catawba,
Cherokee, Clay, Cleveland, Davidson,
Davie, Forsyth, Gaston, Graham,
Guilford, Haywood, Henderson, Iredell,
Jackson, Lincoln, Macon, Madison,
McDowell, Mecklenburg, Mitchell,
Montgomery, Polk, Randolph,
Richmond, Rockingham, Rowan,
Rutherford, Stanly, Stokes, Surry,
Transylvania, Union, Watauga, Wilkes,
Yadkin, and Yancey counties.

Raleigh-Durham Field Office
301 Roycroft Drive
Durham, NC 27703
This office serves Alamance, Beaufort,
Bertie, Bladen, Brunswick, Camden,
Carteret, Caswell, Chathan, Chowan,
Columbus, Craven, Cumberland,
Currituck, Dare, Duplin, Durham,
Edgecombe, Franklin, Gates, Granville,
Greene, Halifax, Harnett, Hertford,
Hoke, Hyde, Johnston, Jones, Lee,
Lenoir, Martin, Moore, Nash, New
Hanover, Northhampton, Onslow,
Orange, Pamlico, Pasquotank, Pender,

Perquimans, Person, Pitt, Robeson, Sampson, Scotland, Tyrrell, Vance, Wake, Warren, Washington, Wayne, and Wilson counties.

NORTH DAKOTA
St. Paul Field Office
2901 Metro Drive, Suite 100
Bloomington, MN 55425.
In addition to serving the states of North Dakota, South Dakota, and Minnesota, this office also serves over 30 counties in western Wisconsin.

OHIO
Cincinnati Field Office
J.W. Peck Federal Building
550 Main Street, Room 4001
Cincinnati, OH 45202-5298
This office is closed on Wednesdays.
This office serves Adams, Brown, Butler, Champaign, Clark, Clermont, Clinton, Darke, Greene, Hamilton, Highland, Lawrence, Miami, Montgomery, Preble, Scioto, Shelby, and Warren counties.

Cleveland Field Office
A.J.C. Federal Building
1240 East 9th Street, Room 501
Cleveland, OH 44199
This office is closed on Wednesdays.
This office serves Allen, Ashland, Ashtabula, Auglaize, Carroll, Columbiana, Crawford, Cuyahoga, Defiance, Erie, Fulton, Geauga, Hancock, Hardin, Henry, Holmes, Huron, Lake, Lorain, Lucas, Mahoning, Marion, Medina, Mercer, Ottawa, Paulding, Portage, Putnam, Richland, Ross, Sandusky, Seneca, Stark, Summit, Trumbull, Tuscarawas, Union, Van Wert, Wayne, Williams, Wood, and Wyandot counties.

Columbus Field Office
Leveque Tower
50 West Broad Street, Suite 306
Columbus, OH 43215
The information unit is closed on Wednesdays.
This office serves the following counties in Ohio: Athens, Belmont, Coshocton, Delaware, Fairfield, Fayette, Franklin, Gallia, Guernsey, Harrison, Hocking, Jackson, Jefferson, Knox, Licking, Logan, Madison, Meigs, Monroe, Morgan, Morrow, Muskingum, Noble, Perry, Pickaway, Pike, Ross, Union, Vinton, and Washington.

OKLAHOMA
Oklahoma City Field Office
4400 Southwest 44th Street, Suite A
Oklahoma City, Oklahoma 73119
This office is closed for InfoPass appointments on Wednesdays.

OREGON
Portland Field Office
511 NW Broadway, Room 117
Portland, OR 97209
The information center is open Monday, Tuesday, Thursday, and Friday from 7:30 A.M. until 11:30 A.M. and from 1:10 P.M. until 4 P.M. The office is closed on Wednesday, Saturday, and Sunday. The InfoPass kiosk in the information lobby is available for use Monday to Friday between 7:30 A.M. and 4:30 P.M.

PENNSYLVANIA
Philadelphia Field Office
1600 Callowhill Street
Philadelphia, PA 19130
This office serves Adams, Berks, Bradford, Bucks, Cameron, Carbon, Centre, Chester, Clinton, Columbia,

Cumberland, Dauphin, Delaware, Franklin, Fulton, Huntingdon, Juniata, Lackawana, Lancaster, Lebanon, Lehigh, Luzerne, Lycoming, Mifflin, Monroe, Montgomery, Montour, Northampton, Northumberland, Perry, Philadelphia, Pike, Potter, Schuylkill, Snyder, Sullivan, Susquehanna, Tioga, Union, Wayne, Wyoming, and York counties.

Pittsburgh Field Office
3000 Sidney Street, Suite 200
Pittsburgh, PA 15203
This office serves the state of West Virginia and the following counties in Pennsylvania: Allegheny, Armstrong, Beaver, Bedford, Blair, Butler, Cambria, Clarion, Clearfield, Crawford, Elk, Erie, Fayette, Forest, Greene, Indiana, Jefferson, Lawrence, McKean, Mercer, Somerset, Venango, Warren, Washington, and Westmoreland.

PUERTO RICO
San Juan Field Office
San Patricio Office Center
7 Tabonuco Street, Suite 100
Guaynabo, PR 00968

RHODE ISLAND
Providence Field Office
200 Dyer Street
Providence, RI 02903
This office is closed on the third Friday of each month.

SOUTH CAROLINA
Charleston Field Office
1 Poston Road, Suite 130
Park Shore Center
Charleston, SC 29407
This office serves the state of South Carolina.

Greer Field Office
142-D West Phillips Road
Greer, SC 29650
This office serves the following counties in South Carolina: Abbeville, Anderson, Cherokee, Chester, Edgefield, Fairfield, Greenville, Greenwood, Lancaster, Laurens, McCormick, Newberry, Oconee, Pickens, Saluda, Spartanburg, Union, and York.

SOUTH DAKOTA
St. Paul Field Office
2901 Metro Drive, Suite 100
Bloomington, MN 55425
This office serves the states of North Dakota, South Dakota and Minnesota. In addition, this office also serves 30 counties in western Wisconsin.

TENNESSEE
Memphis Field Office
842 Virginia Run Cove
Memphis, TN 38122
This office serves the state of Tennessee.
In addition, this office serves over 40 counties in Arkansas and 36 counties in Mississippi.

TEXAS
Dallas Field Office
8101 North Stemmons Freeway (Interstate 35)
Dallas, TX 75247
This office is closed to the public on Wednesdays.
This office serves the cities of Dallas, Fort Worth, and Irving and the following counties: Anderson, Andrews, Archer, Armstrong, Baily, Baylor, Borden, Bosque, Bowie, Briscoe, Callahan, Camp, Carson, Cass, Castro, Cherokee, Childress, Clay, Cochran,

Collin, Collingsworth, Comanche, Cooke, Cottle, Crosby, Dallam, Dallas, Dawson, Deaf Smith, Delta, Denton, Dickens, Donley, Eastland, Ellis, Erath, Fannin, Fisher, Floyd, Foard, Franklin, Freestone, Gaines, Garza, Gray, Grayson, Gregg, Hale, Hall, Hamilton, Hansford, Hardeman, Harison, Hartley, Haskell, Hemphill, Henderson, Hill, Hockley, Hood, Hopkins, Houston, Howard, Hunt, Hutchison, Jack, Johnson, Jones, Kautman, Kent, King, Knox, Lamar, Lamb, Leon, Limestone, Lipscomb, Lubbock, Lynn, Marion, Martin, Mitchell, Montague, Moore, Morris, Motley, Navarro, Nolan, Ochiltree, Oldham, Palo Pinto, Panola, Parker, Parmer, Potter, Rains, Randall, Red River, Roberts, Rockwall, Rusk, Scurry, Shackelford, Sherman, Smith, Somervell, Stephens, Stonewall, Swisher, Tarrant, Taylor, Terry, Throckmorton, Titus, Upshur, Van Zandt, Wheeler, Wichita, Willbarger, Wise, Wood, Yoakum, and Young.

El Paso Field Office

1545 Hawkins Boulevard
El Paso, TX 79925
This office is closed on Wednesdays.
This office serves the Texas counties of El Paso and Odessa-Midland as well as these counties in southern New Mexico: Chavez, Dona Ana, Eddy, Grant, Hidalgo, Lea, Lincoln, Luna, Otero, and Sierra.

Harlingen Field Office

1717 Zoy Street
Harlingen, TX 78552
This office is closed on Wednesdays.
This office serves the counties of Brooks, Cameron, Hidalgo, Kenedy, Kleberg, Starr, and Willacy.

Houston Field Office

126 Northpoint Drive
Houston, TX 77060
This office serves the counties of Angelina, Austin, Brazoria, Chambers, Colorado, Fort Bend, Galveston, Grimes, Hardin, Harris, Jasper, Jefferson, Liberty, Madison, Matagorda, Montgomery, Nacodogches, Newton, Orange, Polk, Sabine, San Augustin, San Jacinto, Shelby, Trinity, Tyler, Walker, Waller, Washington, and Wharton.

San Antonio Field Office

8940 Fourwinds Drive
San Antonio, TX 78239
This office serves the following counties: Aransas, Atascosa, Bandera, Bastrop, Bee, Bell, Bexar, Blanco, Brazos, Brooks, Brown, Burleson, Burnet, Caldwell, Calhoun, Coke, Coleman, Comal, Concho, Coryell, Crockett, De Witt, Dimmitt, Duval, Edwards, Falls, Fayette, Frio, Gillespie, Glasscock, Goliad, Gonzales, Guadalupe, Hays, Irion, Jackson, Jim Hogg, Jim Wells, Karnes, Kendall, Kerr, Kimble, Kinney, Lampasas, La Salle, Lavaca, Lee, Live Oak, Llano, McCulloch, McLennan, Mason, Maverick, Medina, Menard, Milam, Mills, Nueces, Reagan, Real, Refugio, Robertson, Runnels, San Patricio, San Saba, Schleicher, Sterling, Sutton, Tom Green, Travis, Uvalde, Val Verde, Victoria, Webb, Williamson, Wilson, Zapata, and Zavala.

UTAH
Salt Lake City Field Office

5272 South College Drive, Suite 100
Salt Lake City, UT 84123

VERMONT
Saint Albans Field Office
64 Gricebrook Road
Saint Albans, VT 05478

VIRGINIA
Norfolk Field Office
Norfolk Commerce Park
5280 Henneman Drive
Norfolk, VA 23513
This office serves these counties in
Virginia, as well as the independent
cities that are in the area near these
counties: Accomack, Amelia, Brunswick,
Caroline, Charles City, Chesterfield,
Dinwiddie, Essex, Gloucester,
Goochland, Greensville, Hanover,
Henrico, Isle of Wright, James City, King
and Queen, King William, Lancaster,
Louisa, Lunenburg, Mathews,
Mecklenburg, Middlesex, New Kent,
Northampton, Northumberland,
Nottoway, Powhatan, Prince Edward,
Prince George, Richmond,
Southampton, Spotsylvania, Surry,
Sussex, Westmoreland, and York.
Some counties are served by the
Washington, DC office.

VIRGIN ISLANDS
Charlotte Amalie Field Office
8000 Nisky Center, Suite 1A
Charlotte Amalie
St. Thomas, VI 00802
The Information Unit is closed on Fridays.
This office serves St. Thomas, St. John,
and Water Island, U.S. Virgin Islands.

Christiansted, Saint Croix Field Office
Sunny Isle Shopping Center, Suite 5A
Christiansted, Saint Croix
USVI 00823
This office serves all of Saint Croix and
the U.S. Virgin Islands.

WASHINGTON
Seattle Field Office
12500 Tukwila International Boulevard
Seattle, WA 98168
This office is closed for InfoPass
appointments on Fridays.
This office serves these counties in
Washington: Clallam, Clark, Cowlitz,
Grays Harbor, Island, Jefferson, King,
Kitsap, Lewis, Mason, Pacific, Pierce,
San Juan, Skagit, Skamania,
Snohomish, Thurston, Wahkiakum,
and Whatcom.

Spokane Field Office
U.S. Courthouse
920 West Riverside, Room 691
Spokane, WA 99201
If you are unable to schedule an appoint-
ment using InfoPass, you may send an
appointment request by mail to USCIS,
U.S. Courthouse, 920 West Riverside,
Spokane, WA 99201.
This office is closed on Fridays.
The office serves these counties in
Washington: Adams, Asotin, Columbia,
Ferry, Garfield, Lincoln, Okanogan,
Pend O'Reille, Spokane, Stevens,
Walla Walla, and Whitman.
This office also serves ten counties in
Idaho.

Yakima Field Office
415 North Third Street
Yakima, WA 98901
If you do not have access to the Internet,
appointments may be scheduled using
the InfoPass kiosk located in the
Yakima Field Office.
This office serves these counties in
Washington: Benton, Chelan, Douglas,
Franklin, Grant, Kittitas, Klickitat, and
Yakima.

WASHINGTON, DC (See District of Columbia.)

WEST VIRGINIA
Charleston Field Office
210 Kanawha Boulevard West
Charleston, WV 25302
If you are in the Charleston satellite office's jurisdiction, but you live closer to the Pittsburgh field office, you may schedule an InfoPass appointment to visit the Pittsburgh field office.

Pittsburgh Field Office
3000 Sidney Street, Suite 200
Pittsburgh, PA 15203
This office serves the state of West Virginia and 25 counties in Pennsylvania.

WISCONSIN
Milwaukee Field Office
310 East Knapp Street
Milwaukee, WI 53202
This office is closed on Fridays.
This office serves these counties in eastern Wisconsin: Brown, Calumet, Columbia, Crawford, Dane, Dodge, Door, Florence, Fond Du Lac, Forest, Grant, Green, Greeen Lake, Iowa, Jefferson, Kenosha, Kewaunee, Lafayette, Langlade, Manitowoc, Marinette, Marquette, Menominee, Milwaukee, Oconto, Outgamie, Ozaukee, Racine, Richland, Rock, Sauk, Shawano, Sheboygan, Walworth, Washington, Waukesha, Waupaca, Waushara, and Winnebago.

St. Paul Field Office
2901 Metro Drive, Suite 100
Bloomington, MN 55425
This office serves the states of North Dakota, South Dakota and Minnesota. This office also serves these counties in western Wisconsin: Ashland, Adams, Barron, Bayfield, Buffalo, Burnett, Chippewa, Clark, Douglas, Dunn, Eau Claire, Iron, Jackson, Juneau, La Crosse, Lincoln, Madeline Island, Marathon, Monroe, Oneida, Pepin, Pierce, Polk, Portage, Price, Rusk, Saint Croix, Sawyer, Taylor, Trempeleau, Vernon, Vilas, Washburn, and Wood.

WYOMING
Casper Field Office
150 East B Street, Room 1014
Casper, WY 82601
To receive service at this location, you must have an appointment that has been scheduled by USCIS.
Until further notice, customers, who would normally make an InfoPass appointment at the office in Casper, Wyoming, should, instead, schedule their InfoPass appointments at the Denver Field Office (see next entry).
This office serves Big Horn, Campbell, Converse, Crook, Fremont, Hot Springs, Johnson, Natrona, Niobrara, Park, Sheridan, Sublette, Teton, Washakie, and Weston counties.

Denver Field Office
4730 Paris Street
Denver, CO 80239
This office serves Colorado and Wyoming.

Resources

1. The best and easiest way to get more **information about the USCIS** is by using the computer. If you don't have a computer, but feel comfortable using one, most public libraries in the United States and many abroad offer them. If you would rather call, the customer service number is 800-375-5283. The hearing impaired TTY customer service number is 800-767-1833.

2. The USCIS offers a useful and usable **booklet,** *Welcome to the United States: A Guide for New Immigrants* (booklet number **M-618**). You can download this 124-page guide at www.uscis.gov in English, Spanish, Chinese, Vietnamese, Tagalog, Korean, Russian, Arabic, French, Portuguese, and Haitian Creole.

3. To get the monthly **Visa Bulletin** from the Bureau of Consular Affairs, Department of State, go to http://travel.state.gov/visa/ visa_1750.html. On the home page, select the VISA section, where you'll find the Visa Bulletin.

    You can get your name and e-mail address on the Department of State's e-mail subscription list for the Visa Bulletin. Send an e-mail to listserv@calist.state.gov. In your message section, type:

    Subscribe Visa-Bulletin   Your first name and last name

If you want to stop receiving the bulletin, send an e-mail message to listscrv@calist.state.gov. In the message, type Signoff Visa Bulletin.

If you have a question about the Visa Bulletin, e-mail VisaBulletin@state.gov. You can also call the Department of State Visa Office to hear a recorded message with visa cutoff dates and which priority dates are being worked on. The number is 202-663-1541. The recording is usually updated by the middle of each month with information on cutoff dates for the following month.

4. **For general visa questions**, you will probably find answers to most of your questions on the websites of the USCIS or the Department of State, though you will have to be patient and careful.

If you e-mail a question, it may be a while (more than a day) before you receive an answer. You are likely one of thousands who are writing.

On the subject line of the message, tell exactly what you are writing about.

Example: spouse visa; affidavit of support; petition for relative

In your message, don't tell a story. Just give the facts and briefly tell why you are writing.

5. If your question is about a visa case that is being **processed in another country**, contact the U.S. embassy or consulate there. Officials there will have the information about your case.

6. The **National Visa Center** is at 32 Rochester Avenue, Portsmouth, New Hampshire 03801-2909. Contact it only if you have a change of address or need to give other important changes in your life that may affect your visa. For a **full glossary** (list) of visa terms, go to http://travel.state.gov/visa.

7. The DOS offers a helpful and engaging little book for parents seeking to **adopt abroad**, *Intercountry Adoption From A-Z*. You can download it from the DOS Intercountry Adoption page at http://adoption.state.gov/.

Fees and Forms

Fees change. Paying the wrong fees causes delays. To make sure you are paying the right fees, go to www.uscis.gov or call customer service. Or visit the U.S. consulate in your country to check what the fees are at the time you are filing.

Some fees must be paid to National Visa Center (NVC) services. The National Visa Center sends bills for certain fees during the visa process. The bill for processing the I-864, Affidavit of Support, is sent to the petitioner. The bill for immigrant visa processing goes to the applicant's agent. Along with the bills, the NVC sends an addressed return envelope. You *must* use this envelope when you pay the fees. You must also:

◆ Place the correct postage (stamps) on the envelope.
◆ Pay the bill only when the NVC tells you to do so.
◆ Send the envelope to the address on it. Payments shouldn't be sent to the NVC at Portsmouth, New Hampshire.

Never send cash. Pay fees by personal check or money order unless only a money order is asked for. It is best to use a separate check for each payment. You may, for example, be sending two different forms, each of which has a fee. Pay to the order of "The Department of

Homeland Security" unless you are told otherwise. Your payment should have your name and address on the front. It should have your A (Alien) number on it in case it gets separated from other paperwork. And always make copies.

Sample Fee Chart

Here are examples of fees from 2009. You must check fees before sending your forms because they may change.

Purpose	Fee
Immigrant visa application processing fee (per person)	$355
Diversity Visa Lottery surcharge for immigrant visa application (per person)	$375
Affidavit of Support Review (only when AOS is reviewed domestically), Form I-864	$ 70
Application for Determining Returning Resident Status, Form DSP-117	$400
Fingerprinting	$ 85

Sample Forms

Following are forms like those you may soon be filling out. The more familiar you are with them, the better. These forms change from time to time. Be careful—make sure the ones you actually fill out are the most recent. If you're downloading them from a computer, do so only from the official NSCIS or DOS sites. Like all official sites, they end in .gov. Other sites that aren't official may have older, out-of-date forms.

The U.S. government is fussy about how forms are filled out. They must be correct. They must be clear. They must be neat, with no mistakes or crossed-out words. Be completely truthful in your answers. Answer every question even if the answer is one you would rather not give. Your form will be sent back to you if you leave anything out or if information is incorrect. Remember to sign each form. You may not get a chance at another time to fix what you've written. And, anyway, you won't want to create reasons for delays.

The forms may have questions that you think you cannot answer.

If you don't have the information, because it . . . answer

doesn't exist (such as a middle name)	none
doesn't apply to you (do you have children?)	no
is not applicable (what are the children's names?)	n/a

Some Forms You May Need

Form Number   Purpose

Form Number	Purpose
I-90	Replacement or renewal of Permanent Resident Card
I-129F	Petition for Alien Fiance(e)*
I-130	Petition for Alien Relative*
I-131	Application for Travel Document*
I-134	Affidavit of Support
I-140	Petition for Alien Worker
I-360	Petition for Amerasian, Widow(er), Special Immigrant
I-485	Application to Register Permanent Resident or Adjust Status
I-526	Petition by Alien Entrepreneurs
I-529	Petition by Entrepreneur to Remove Conditions
I-800	Classification of orphan adoption
I-693	Medical information*
I-730	Refugee/Asylee Relative Petition
I-765	Request for work permit
DS-230	Application for Visa and Registration
DSP-117	Application To Determine Returning Resident Status
ETA 750	Labor certification
G-325A	Biographic Information*

An asterisk (*) indicates that a sample follows.

Department of Homeland Security
U.S. Citizenship and Immigration Services

I-129F, Petition for Alien Fiancé(e)

Do not write in these blocks. For USCIS Use Only

Case ID #	Action Block	Fee Stamp
A #		
G-28 #		

The petition is approved for status under Section 101(a)(5)(k). It is valid for four months from the date of action. _____

AMCON:

- [ ] Personal Interview
- [ ] Previously Forwarded
- [ ] Document Check
- [ ] Field Investigation

Remarks:

Part A. Start Here. Information about you.

1. Name *(Family name in CAPS)* *(First)* *(Middle)*

2. Address *(Number and Street)* Apt. #

(Town or City) *(State or Country)* *(Zip/Postal Code)*

3. Place of Birth *(Town or City)* *(State/Country)*

4. Date of Birth *(mm/dd/yyyy)*   **5. Gender**
- [ ] Male [ ] Female

6. Marital Status
- [ ] Married [ ] Single [ ] Widowed [ ] Divorced

7. Other Names Used *(including maiden name)*

8a. U.S. Social Security Number 8b. A# *(if any)*

9. Names of Prior Spouses   Date(s) Marriage(s) Ended

10. My citizenship was acquired through *(check one)*
- [ ] Birth in the U.S. [ ] Naturalization

Give number of certificate, date and place it was issued.

- [ ] Parents

Have you obtained a certificate of citizenship in your name?
- [ ] Yes [ ] No

If "Yes," give certificate number, date and place it was issued.

11. Have you ever filed for this or any other alien fiancé(e) or husband/wife before?
- [ ] Yes [ ] No

If "Yes," give name of all aliens, place and date of filing, A# and result. *(Attached additional sheets as necessary.)*

Part B. Information about your alien fiancé(e).

1. Name *(Family name in CAPS)* *(First)* *(Middle)*

2. Address *(Number and Street)* Apt. #

(Town or City) *(State or Country)* *(Zip/Postal Code)*

3a. Place of Birth *(Town or City)* *(State/Country)*

3b. Country of Citizenship

4. Date of Birth *(mm/dd/yyyy)*   **5. Gender**
- [ ] Male [ ] Female

6. Marital Status
- [ ] Married [ ] Single [ ] Widowed [ ] Divorced

7. Other Names Used *(including maiden name)*

8. U.S. Social Security #   9. A# *(if any)*

10. Names of Prior Spouses   Date(s) Marriage(s) Ended

11. Has your fiancé(e) ever been in the U.S.?
- [ ] Yes [ ] No

12. If your fiancé(e) is currently in the U.S., complete the following:

He or she last arrived as a:*(visitor, student, exchange alien, crewman, stowaway, temporary worker, without inspection, etc.)*

Arrival/Departure Record (I-94) Number

Date of Arrival *(mm/dd/yy)*   **Date authorized stay expired, or will expire as shown on I-94 or I-95**

INITIAL RECEIPT _____ RESUBMITTED _____ RELOCATED: Rec'd _____ Sent _____ COMPLETED: Appv'd. _____ Denied _____ Ret'd. _____

Form I-129F (Rev. 07/30/07) Y

Part B. **Information about your alien fiancé(e).** *(Continued.)*

13. List all children of your alien fiancé(e) *(if any)*

Name *(First/Middle/Last)*	Date of Birth *(mm/dd/yyyy)*	Country of Birth	Present Address

14. Address in the United States where your fiancé(e) intends to live.

(Number and Street)   (Town or City)   (State)

15. Your fiancé(e)'s address abroad.

(Number and Street)   (Town or City)   (State or Province)

(Country)   (Phone Number; Include Country, City and Area Codes)

16. If your fiancé(e)'s native alphabet uses other than Roman letters, write his or her name and address abroad in the native alphabet.

(Name)   (Number and Street)

(Town or City)   (State or Province)   (Country)

17. Is your fiancé(e) related to you?   ☐ Yes   ☐ No

If you are related, state the nature and degree of relationship, e.g., third cousin or maternal uncle, etc.

18. Has your fiancé(e) met and seen you within the two-year period immediately receding the filing of this petition?

☐ Yes   ☐ No

Describe the circumstances under which you met. If you have not personally met each other, explain how the relationship was established. If you met your fiancé(e) or spouse though an international marriage broker, please explain those circumstances in Question 19 below. Explain also in detail any reasons you may have for requesting that the requirement that you and your fiancé(e) must have met should not apply to you.

19. Did you meet your fiancé(e) or spouse through the services of an international marriage broker?

☐ Yes   ☐ No

If you answered yes, please provide the name and any contact information you may have (including internet or street address) of the international marriage broker and where the international marriage broker is located. Attach additional sheets of paper if necessary.

20. Your fiancé(e) will apply for a visa abroad at the American embassy or consulate at:

(City)   (Country)

NOTE: (Designation of a U.S. embassy or consulate outside the country of your fiancé(e)'s last residence does not guarantee acceptance for processing by that foreign post. Acceptance is at the discretion of the designated embassy or consulate.)

Part C. Other information.

1. If you are serving overseas in the Armed Forces of the United States, please answer the following:

I presently reside or am stationed overseas and my current mailing address is:

2. Have you ever been convicted by a court of law (civil or criminal) or court martialed by a military tribunal for any of the following crimes:

- Domestic violence, sexual assault, child abuse and neglect, dating violence, elder abuse or stalking. (Please refer to page 3 of the instructions for the full definition of the term "domestic violence.)

- Homicide, murder, manslaughter, rape, abusive sexual contact, sexual exploitation, incest, torture, trafficking, peonage, holding hostage, involuntary servitude, slave trade, kidnapping, abduction, unlawful criminal restraint, false imprisonment or an attempt to commit any of these crimes, or

- Three or more convictions for crimes relating to a controlled substance or alcohol not arising from a single act.

☐ Yes ☐ No

Answering this question is required even if your records were sealed or otherwise cleared or if anyone, including a judge, law enforcement officer, or attorney, told you that you no longer have a record. Using a separate sheet(s) of paper, attach information relating to the conviction(s), such as crime involved, date of conviction and sentence.

3. If you have provided information about a conviction for a crime listed above and you were being battered or subjected to extreme cruelty by your spouse, parent, or adult child at the time of your conviction, check all of the following that apply to you:

☐ I was acting in self-defense.

☐ I violated a protection order issued for my own protection.

☐ I committed, was arrested for, was convicted of, or plead guilty to committing a crime that did not result in serious bodily injury, and there was a connection between the crime committed and my having been battered or subjected to extreme cruelty.

Part D. Penalties, certification and petitioner's signature.

PENALTIES: You may by law be imprisoned for not more than five years, or fined $250,000, or both, for entering into a marriage contract for the purpose of evading any provision of the immigration laws, and you may be fined up to $10,000 or imprisoned up to five years, or both, for knowingly and willfully falsifying or concealing a material fact or using any false document in submitting this petition.

YOUR CERTIFICATION: I am legally able to and intend to marry my alien fiancé(e) within 90 days of his or her arrival in the United States. I certify, under penalty of perjury under the laws of the United States of America, that the foregoing is true and correct. Furthermore, I authorize the release of any information from my records that U.S. Citizenship and Immigration Services needs to determine eligibility for the benefit that I am seeking.

Moreover, I understand that this petition, including any criminal conviction information that I am required to provide with this petition, as well as any related criminal background information pertaining to me that U.S. Citizenship and Immigration Services may discover independently in adjudicating this petition will be disclosed to the beneficiary of this petition.

Signature	Date *(mm/dd/yyyy)*	Daytime Telephone Number *(with area code)*

E-Mail Address (if any)

Part E. Signature of person preparing form, if other than above. *(Sign below.)*

I declare that I prepared this application at the request of the petitioner and it is based on all information of which I have knowledge.

Signature	Print or Type Your Name	G-28 ID Number	Date *(mm/dd/yyyy)*

Firm Name and Address	Daytime Telephone Number *(with area code)*
	E-Mail Address (if any)

Form I-129F (Rev. 07/30/07) Y Page 3

OMB #1615-0012; Expires 01/31/11

I-130, Petition for Alien Relative

DO NOT WRITE IN THIS BLOCK - FOR USCIS OFFICE ONLY

A#	Action Stamp	Fee Stamp

Section of Law/Visa Category
- ☐ 201(b) Spouse - IR-1/CR-1
- ☐ 201(b) Child - IR-2/CR-2
- ☐ 201(b) Parent - IR-5
- ☐ 203(a)(1) Unm. S or D - F1-1
- ☐ 203(a)(2)(A)Spouse - F2-1
- ☐ 203(a)(2)(A) Child - F2-2
- ☐ 203(a)(2)(B) Unm. S or D - F2-4
- ☐ 203(a)(3) Married S or D - F3-1
- ☐ 203(a)(4) Brother/Sister - F4-1

Petition was filed on: _____ (priority date)
- ☐ Personal Interview
- ☐ Pet. ☐ Ben. "A" File Reviewed
- ☐ Field Investigation
- ☐ 203(a)(2)(A) Resolved
- ☐ Previously Forwarded
- ☐ I-485 Filed Simultaneously
- ☐ 204(g) Resolved
- ☐ 203(g) Resolved

Remarks:

A. Relationship   You are the petitioner. Your relative is the beneficiary.

1. I am filing this petition for my:
☐ Husband/Wife ☐ Parent ☐ Brother/Sister ☐ Child

2. Are you related by adoption?
☐ Yes ☐ No

3. Did you gain permanent residence through adoption?
☐ Yes ☐ No

B. Information about you

1. Name (Family name in CAPS) (First) (Middle)

2. Address (Number and Street) (Apt. No.)

(Town or City) (State/Country) (Zip/Postal Code)

3. Place of Birth (Town or City) (State/Country)

4. Date of Birth

5. Gender ☐ Male ☐ Female

6. Marital Status ☐ Married ☐ Single ☐ Widowed ☐ Divorced

7. Other Names Used (including maiden name)

8. Date and Place of Present Marriage (if married)

9. U.S. Social Security Number (If any)   **10. Alien Registration Number**

11. Name(s) of Prior Husband(s)/Wive(s)   **12. Date(s) Marriage(s) Ended**

13. If you are a U.S. citizen, complete the following:

My citizenship was acquired through (check one):
- ☐ Birth in the U.S.
- ☐ Naturalization. Give certificate number and date and place of issuance.

- ☐ Parents. Have you obtained a certificate of citizenship in your own name?
  ☐ Yes. Give certificate number, date and place of issuance. ☐ No

14. If you are a lawful permanent resident alien, complete the following:
Date and place of admission for or adjustment to lawful permanent residence and class of admission.

14b. Did you gain permanent resident status through marriage to a U.S. citizen or lawful permanent resident?
☐ Yes ☐ No

C. Information about your relative

1. Name (Family name in CAPS) (First) (Middle)

2. Address (Number and Street) (Apt. No.)

(Town or City) (State/Country) (Zip/Postal Code)

3. Place of Birth (Town or City) (State/Country)

4. Date of Birth

5. Gender ☐ Male ☐ Female

6. Marital Status ☐ Married ☐ Single ☐ Widowed ☐ Divorced

7. Other Names Used (including maiden name)

8. Date and Place of Present Marriage (if married)

9. U.S. Social Security Number (If any)   **10. Alien Registration Number**

11. Name(s) of Prior Husband(s)/Wive(s)   **12. Date(s) Marriage(s) Ended**

13. Has your relative ever been in the U.S.? ☐ Yes ☐ No

14. If your relative is currently in the U.S., complete the following:
He or she arrived as a:
(visitor, student, stowaway, without inspection, etc.)

Arrival/Departure Record (I-94)   Date arrived

Date authorized stay expired, or will expire, as shown on Form I-94 or I-95

15. Name and address of present employer (if any)

Date this employment began

16. Has your relative ever been under immigration proceedings?
☐ No ☐ Yes Where _____ When _____
☐ Removal ☐ Exclusion/Deportation ☐ Rescission ☐ Judicial Proceedings

INITIAL RECEIPT   RESUBMITTED   RELOCATED: Rec'd   Sent   COMPLETED: Appv'd   Denied   Ret'd

Form I-130 (Rev. 05/27/08)Y

C. Information about your alien relative (continued)

17. List husband/wife and all children of your relative.

(Name)	(Relationship)	(Date of Birth)	(Country of Birth)

18. Address in the United States where your relative intends to live.

(Street Address)	(Town or City)	(State)

19. Your relative's address abroad. (Include street, city, province and country)   Phone Number (if any)

20. If your relative's native alphabet is other than Roman letters, write his or her name and foreign address in the native alphabet.

(Name)   Address (Include street, city, province and country):

21. If filing for your husband/wife, give last address at which you lived together. (Include street, city, province, if any, and country):

From: To:

22. Complete the information below if your relative is in the United States and will apply for adjustment of status.

Your relative is in the United States and will apply for adjustment of status to that of a lawful permanent resident at the USCIS office in:

If your relative is not eligible for adjustment of status, he or she will apply for a visa abroad at the American consular post in:

(City)	(State)	(City)	(Country)

NOTE: Designation of a U.S. embassy or consulate outside the country of your relative's last residence does not guarantee acceptance for processing by that post. Acceptance is at the discretion of the designated embassy or consulate.

D. Other information

1. If separate petitions are also being submitted for other relatives, give names of each and relationship.

2. Have you ever before filed a petition for this or any other alien? ☐ Yes ☐ No

If "Yes," give name, place and date of filing and result.

WARNING: USCIS investigates claimed relationships and verifies the validity of documents. USCIS seeks criminal prosecutions when family relationships are falsified to obtain visas.

PENALTIES: By law, you may be imprisoned for not more than five years or fined $250,000, or both, for entering into a marriage contract for the purpose of evading any provision of the immigration laws. In addition, you may be fined up to $10,000 and imprisoned for up to five years, or both, for knowingly and willfully falsifying or concealing a material fact or using any false document in submitting this petition.

YOUR CERTIFICATION: I certify, under penalty of perjury under the laws of the United States of America, that the foregoing is true and correct. Furthermore, I authorize the release of any information from my records that U.S. Citizenship and Immigration Services needs to determine eligiblity for the benefit that I am seeking.

E. Signature of petitioner.

Date   Phone Number (   )

F. Signature of person preparing this form, if other than the petitioner.

I declare that I prepared this document at the request of the person above and that it is based on all information of which I have any knowledge.

Print Name _____   Signature _____   Date _____

Address _____   G-28 ID or VOLAG Number, if any. _____

INSTRUCTIONS

What Is the Purpose of This Form?

This form is used to apply to the Bureau of Citizenship and Immigration Services (CIS), comprised of offices of the former Immigration and Naturalization Service (INS), for the following travel documents:

- **Reentry Permit** - A reentry permit allows a permanent resident or conditional resident to apply for admission to the United States upon return from abroad during the permit's validity, without having to obtain a returning resident visa from a U.S. embassy or consulate.

- **Refugee Travel Document** - A refugee travel document is issued to a person classified as a refugee or asylee, or to a permanent resident who obtained such status as a result of being a refugee or asylee in the United States. Persons who hold such status must have a refugee travel document to return to the United States after temporary travel abroad unless he or she is in possession of a valid advance parole document. A refugee travel document is issued by the CIS to implement Article 28 of the United Nations Convention of July 28, 1951.

- **Advance Parole Document** - An advance parole document is issued solely to authorize the temporary parole of a person into the United States. The document may be accepted by a transportation company in lieu of a visa as an authorization for the holder to travel to the United States. An advance parole document is not issued to serve in place of any required passport.

Advance parole is an extraordinary measure used sparingly to bring an otherwise inadmissible alien to the United States for a temporary period of time due to a compelling emergency. Advance parole cannot be used to circumvent the normal visa issuing procedures and is not a means to bypass delays in visa issuance.

NOTE: If you are in the United States and wish to travel abroad, you do not need to apply for advance parole if both conditions described below in numbers **1** and **2** are met:

1. You are in one of the following nonimmigrant categories:

    a. An H-1, temporary worker, or H-4, spouse or child of an H-1; **or**

    b. An L-1, intracompany transferee, or L-2, spouse or child of an L-1; **or**

    c. A K-3, spouse, or K-4, child, of a U.S. citizen; **or**

    d. A V-2, spouse, or V-3, child, of a lawful permanent resident; **and**

2. A Form I-485, Application to Register Permanent Residence or Adjust Status, was filed on your behalf and is pending with the CIS.

However, upon returning to the United States, you must present your valid H, L, K or V nonimmigrant visa and continue to remain eligible for that status.

Who May File This Form?

Each applicant must file a separate application for a travel document.

I. Reentry Permit.

A. *If you are in the United States* as a permanent resident or conditional permanent resident, you may apply for a reentry permit.

Departure from the United States before a decision is made on an application for a reentry permit does not affect the application.

You must be physically present in the United States when you file the application. However, a reentry permit may be sent to a U.S. embassy or consulate or Department of Homeland Security (DHS) office abroad for you to pick up, if you request it when you file your application.

With the exception of having to obtain a returning resident visa abroad, a reentry permit does not relieve you of any of the requirements of the United States immigration laws.

If you stay outside the United States for less than one year, you are not required to apply for a reentry permit. You may reenter the United States on your Permanent Resident Card (Form I-551).

If you intend to apply in the future for naturalization, absences from the United States for one year or more will generally break the continuity of your required continuous residence in the United States. If you intended to remain outside the United States for one year or more, you should file a Form N-470, Application to Preserve Residence for Naturalization Purposes. For further information, contact your local CIS office.

B. *Validity of reentry permit.*

1. Generally, a reentry permit issued to a permanent resident shall be valid for two years from the date of issuance. However, if since becoming a permanent resident you have been outside the United States for more than four of the last five years, the permit will be limited to one year, except that a permit with a validity of two years may be issued to the following:

    a. A permanent resident whose travel is on the order of the United States government, other than an exclusion, deportation, removal or recission order.

    b. A permanent resident employed by a public international organization of which the United States is a member by treaty or statute.

    c. A permanent resident who is a professional athlete and regularly competes in the United States and worldwide.

  2. A reentry permit issued to a conditional resident shall be valid for two years from the date of issuance, or to the date the conditional resident must apply for removal of the conditions on his or her status, whichever date comes first.

  3. A reentry permit may not be extended.

C. *A reentry permit may not be issued to you if:*

  1. You have already been issued such a document and it is still valid, unless the prior document has been returned to the CIS, or you can demonstrate that it was lost; **or**

  2. A notice was published in the Federal Register that precludes the issuance of such a document for travel to the area where you intend to go.

NOTICE to permanent or conditional residents who remain outside the United States for more than one year: If you do not obtain a reentry permit and remain outside the United States for one year or more, it may be determined that you have abandoned your permanent or conditional resident status.

II. Refugee Travel Document.

A. *If you are in the United States* in valid refugee or asylee status, or if you are a permanent resident as a direct result of your refugee or asylee status in the United States, you may apply for a refugee travel document. Generally, you must have a refugee travel document to return to the United States after temporary travel abroad.

You must be physically present in the United States when you file the application. However, a refugee travel document may be sent to a United States embassy or consulate or DHS office abroad for you to pick up, if you request it when you file your application.

B. *Validity of refugee travel document.*

  1. A refugee travel document shall be valid for one year.

  2. A refugee travel document may not be extended.

C. *A refugee travel document may not be issued to you if:*

  1. You have already been issued such a document and it is still valid, unless the prior document has been returned to the CIS, or you can demonstrate that it was lost; or

  2. A notice was published in the Federal Register that precludes the issuance of such a document for travel to the area where you intend to go.

NOTICE to permanent residents who obtain permanent residence as a result of their refugee or asylee status: If you do not obtain a reentry permit and remain outside the United States for one year or more, it may be determined that you have abandoned your permanent resident status.

III. Advance Parole Document.

Travel Warning

Before you apply for an advance parole document, read the travel warning carefully.

- If you have been unlawfully present in the United States for more than 180 days but less than one year and you leave before removal proceedings are started against you, you may be inadmissible for three years from the date of departure.

- If you have been unlawfully present in the United States for one year or more, you may be inadmissible for ten years from the date of departure regardless of whether you left before, during or after removal proceedings.

- Unlawful presence is defined as being in the United States without having been inspected and admitted or paroled (illegal entry), or after the period of authorized stay has expired.

- However, certain immigration benefits and time spent in the United States while certain applications are pending may place you in a period of authorized stay. These include, but are not limited to, a properly filed adjustment of status application, temporary protected status (TPS), deferred enforced departure (DED), asylum and withholding of removal.

- Although advance parole may allow you to return to the United States, your departure may trigger the three- or ten-year bar, if you accrued more than 180 days of unlawful presence **BEFORE** the date you were considered to be in a period of authorized stay.

- Therefore, if you apply for adjustment of status after you return to the United States, resume an adjustment application that was pending before you left, or return to a status that requires you to establish that you are not inadmissible, you will need to apply for and receive a waiver of inadmissibility before your adjustment application may be approved or your status continued.

- Generally, only those persons who can establish extreme hardship to their United States citizen or lawful permanent resident spouse or parent may apply for the waiver for humanitarian reasons, to assure family unity or when it is otherwise in the public interest. (See sections 209(c), 212(a)(9) and 244(c) of the Immigration and Nationality Act for more information on unlawful presence and the available waivers.)

A. *If you are outside the United States and need to visit the United States temporarily for emergent humanitarian reasons:*

1. You may apply for an advance parole document. However, your application must be based on the fact that you cannot obtain the necessary visa and any required waiver of inadmissibility. Parole under these conditions is granted on a case-by-case basis for temporary entry, according to such conditions as prescribed.

2. A person in the United States may file this application on your behalf. In so doing, he or she should complete **Part 1** of the form with information about him or herself.

B. *If you are in the United States and seek advance parole:*

1. You may apply if you have an adjustment of status application pending and you seek to travel abroad for emergent personal or bona fide business reasons; or

2. You may apply if you are classified as a refugee or asylee and you seek to travel abroad for emergent personal or bona fide business reasons, or you are traveling to Canada to apply for a U.S. immigrant visa. (See **Part II, Refugee Travel Document on Page of 2 of these Instructions,** for additional information on refugee/asylee travel); or

3. You may apply if you have been granted Temporary Protected Status or another immigration status that allows you to return to that status after a brief, casual and innocent absence (as defined in 8 CFR 244.1) from the United States.

C. *An advance parole document may not be issued to you if:*

1. You held J-1 nonimmigrant status and are subject to the two-year foreign residence requirement as a result of that status; or

2. You are in exclusion, deportation, removal or recission proceedings.

D. *If you travel before the advance parole document is issued, your application will be deemed abandoned if:*

1. You depart from the United States; or

2. The person seeking advance parole attempts to enter the United States before a decision is made on the application.

General Filing Instructions.

Every application must be properly signed and filed with the correct fee. If you are under 14 years of age, your parent or guardian may sign the application on your behalf.

Any applicaton that is not signed or accompanied by the correct fee will be rejected and returned to you. You may correct the deficiency and resubmit the application. However, an application is not considered properly filed until it is accepted by the CIS.

Please answer all questions by typing or clearly printing in black ink. If an item is not applicable to you, write "N/A." If the answer is none, please write "None." If you need extra space to answer a question, attach a separate sheet of paper with your name and A #, if any, written at the top and indicate the number of the question.

Initial Evidence.

I. Evidence of Eligibility.

We may request additional information or evidence, or we may request that you appear at a CIS office for an interview. You must file your application with all the required evidence. If you do not submit the required evidence, it will delay the issuance of the document you are requesting.

All applications must include a **copy of an official photo identity document showing your photo, name and date of birth.** (Example: a valid government issued driver's license, passport identity page, Form I-551, Permanent Resident Card or any other official identity document.) The copy must **clearly** show the photo and identity information. **A Form I-94, Arrival/Departure Document, is not acceptable as a photo identity document.**

If you are applying for a:

A. *Reentry Permit.*

You **must** attach:

1. A copy of the front and back of your Form I-551, Permanent Resident Card; or

2. If you have not yet received your Form I-551, a copy of the biographic page(s) of your passport and a copy of the visa page showing your initial admission as a permanent resident, or other evidence that you are a permanent resident; or

3. A copy of the Form I-797, Notice of Action, approval notice of an application for replacement of your Permanent Resident Card or temporary evidence of permanent resident status.

B. *Refugee Travel Document.*

You **must** attach a copy of the document issued to you by the CIS or former INS showing your refugee or asylee status and the expiration date of such status.

C. *Advance Parole Document.*

1. *If you are in the United States,* you **must** attach:

   a. A copy of any document issued to you by the CIS or former INS showing your present status in the United States; and

   b. An explanation or other evidence showing the circumstances that warrant issuance of an advance parole document; or

c. If you are an applicant for adjustment of status, a copy of the CIS or former INS receipt as evidence that you filed the adjustment application; or

d. If you are traveling to Canada to apply for an immigrant visa, a copy of the U.S. consular appointment letter.

2. *If you are applying for a person who is outside the United States,* you must attach:

a. A statement of how and by whom medical care, transportation, housing, and other expenses and subsistence needs will be met; and

b. An Affidavit of Support (Form I-134), with evidence of the sponsor's occupation and ability to provide necessary support; and

c. A statement explaining why a U.S. visa cannot be obtained, including when and where attempts were made to obtain a visa; and

d. A statement explaining why a waiver of inadmissability cannot be obtained to allow issuance of a visa, including when and where attempts were made to obtain a waiver, and a copy of any CIS or former INS decision on your waiver request; and

e. A copy of any decision on an immigrant petition filed for the person, and evidence regarding any pending immigrant petition; and

f. A complete description of the emergent reasons explaining why advance parole should be authorized and including copies of any evidence you wish considered, and indicating the length of time for which the parole is requested.

II. Photographs.

A. *If you are filing for a reentry permit or a refugee travel document, or if you are in the United States and filing for an advance parole document:*

You must submit two identical color photographs of yourself taken within 30 days of the filing of this application. The photos must have a white background, be printed on thin paper with a glossy finish, and be unmounted and unretouched. **NOTE: Digital photos are not acceptable.**

The photos should show a three-quarter frontal view of the right side of your face, with your right ear visible and your head bare (unless you are wearing a headress as required by a religious order of which you are a member).

The photos should be no larger than 2 by 2 inches. From the top of the head to just below the chin, the image of your head should be about 1 and 1/4 inches. Using a pencil, lightly print your Alien Registration Number (A#), if any, on the back of each photo.

B. *If the person seeking advance parole is outside the United States:*

1. If you are applying for an advance parole document and you are outside the United States, do not submit the photographs with your application. Prior to issuing the parole document, the U.S. embassy or consulate or DHS office abroad will provide you with information regarding the photograph requirements.

2. If you are filing this application for an advance parole document for another person, submit the required photographs of the person to be paroled.

III. Copies.

If these instructions state that a copy of a document may be filed with this application and you choose to send us the original document, we may keep that original for our records. If we request that you submit original documents of any copies, we will return the originals when they are no longer required.

Invalidation of Travel Document.

Any travel document obtained by making a material false representation or concealment in this application will be invalid.

A travel document will also be invalid if you are ordered removed or deported from the United States.

In addition, a refugee travel document will be invalid if the United Nations Convention of July 28, 1951, shall cease to apply or shall not apply to you as provided in Article 1C, D, E or F of the Convention.

Processing Information.

We may request additional information or evidence, or we may request that you appear at a CIS office for an interview. You must file your application with all the required evidence. If you do not submit the required evidence, it will delay the issuance of the document you are requesting. If you do not establish a basis for eligibility, we may deny your application.

Where to File.

A. **If you are applying for a reentry permit or refugee travel document,** mail the application to:

USCIS Nebraska Service Center
P.O. Box 87131
Lincoln, NE 68501-7131

B. **If you are in the United States and filing for an advance parole document:**

1. If you filed at a CIS field office to adjust your status as a permanent resident, submit or mail this application to that office according to its filing procedures.

2. If you filed at a CIS service center to adjust your status as a permanent resident, mail this application to that service center. The service center address is noted on the CIS or former INS receipt related to the filing of your adjustment application. You can also obtain the service center address by visiting the CIS website at www.uscis.gov or calling our National Customer Service Center at 1-800-375-5283.

3. If you were granted Temporary Protected Status, file this application at the local CIS office having jurisdiction over your place of residence.

C. **If you are requesting an advance parole document, and are in removal proceedings or are the beneficiary of a Private Bill,** mail this application to:

USCIS Office of International Affairs
Parole and Humanitarian Assistance Branch
425 "I" Street, N.W.
Attn.: ULLICO Building, 3rd Floor
Washington, DC 20536

D. **If you are outside the United States and applying for an advance parole document on humanitarian grounds, or if such a request is being filed on your behalf,** mail this application to:

USCIS Office of International Affairs
Parole and Humanitarian Assistance Branch
425 "I" Street, N.W.
Attn.: ULLICO Building, 3rd Floor
Washington, DC 20536

E. **Haitian Refugee Immigrant Fairness Act (HRIFA) dependent spouse or child outside the United States:** If you are the spouse or child of a principal HRIFA applicant and are seeking advance parole to enter the United States to file for adjustment of status as a permanent resident, mail this application to:

USCIS Nebraska Service Center
P.O. Box 87131
Lincoln, NE 68501-7131

F. **If you are a refugee or asylee who has filed an adjustment of status application and are now requesting an advance parole document,** mail this application to:

USCIS Nebraska Service Center
P.O. Box 87131
Lincoln, NE 68501-7131

NOTE: If you are a refugee or asylee and have not filed an adjustment of status application, you cannot apply for advance parole. You must request a refugee travel document before departing from the United States. (See instructions on Page 4, "Where to File," item A.)

What Is the Fee?

The fee for this application is $165.00. The fee must be submitted in the exact amount. It cannot be refunded. **Do not mail cash.** All checks and money orders must be drawn on a bank or other financial institution located in the United States and must be payable in United States currency. The check or money order should be made payable to the **U.S. Department of Homeland Security**, unless:

A. If you live in Guam and are filing this application there, make your check or money order payable to the "Treasurer, Guam."

B. If you live in the U.S. Virgin Islands and are filing this application there, make your check or money order payable to the "Commissioner of Finance of the Virgin Islands."

Checks are accepted subject to collection. An uncollected check will render the application and any document issued invalid. A charge of $30.00 will be imposed if a check in payment of a fee is not honored by the bank on which it is drawn.

When making out your check or money order, spell out U.S. Department of Homeland Security. Do not use the initials "USDHS" or "DHS."

What If You Claim Nonresident Alien Status on Your Federal Income Tax Return?

If you are an alien who has established residence in the United States after having been admitted as an immigrant or adjusted status to that of an immigrant, and are considering the filing of a nonresident alien tax return or the non-filing of a tax return on the ground that you are a nonresident alien, you should carefully review the consequences of such actions under the Immigration and Nationality Act.

If you file a nonresident alien tax return or fail to file a tax return, you may be regarded as having abandoned residence in the United States and as having lost your permanent resident status under the Act. As a consequence, you may be ineligible for a visa or other document for which permanent resident aliens are eligible.

You may also be inadmissible to the United States if you seek admission as a returning resident, and you may become ineligible for adjustment of status as a permanent resident or naturalization on the basis of your original entry.

What Are the Penalties for Providing False Information?

If you knowingly and willfully falsify or conceal a material fact or submit a false document with this request, we will deny the benefit you are seeking and may deny any other immigration benefit. In addition, you will face severe penalties provided by law and may be subject to criminal prosecution and/or removal from the United States.

What Is Our Authority for Collecting This Information?

We ask for the information on this form and associated evidence to determine if you have established eligibility for the immigration benefit you are seeking. Our legal right to ask for this information is in 8 U.S.C. 1203 and 1225. We may provide this information to other government agencies. Failure to provide this information and any requested evidence may delay a final decision or result in denial of your request.

Information and CIS Forms.

For information on immigration laws, regulations and procedures and to order CIS forms, call our **National Customer Service Center** toll-free at **1-800-375-5283** or visit our internet web site at **www.uscis.gov**.

Paperwork Reduction Act Notice.

An agency may not conduct or sponsor an information collection and a person is not required to respond to a collection of information unless it contains a currently valid OMB approval number. We try to create forms and instructions that are accurate, can be easily understood and impose the least possible burden on you to provide us with information. Often this is difficult because some immigration laws are very complex. The estimated average time to complete and file this application is as follows: (1) 10 minutes to learn about the law and form; (2) 10 minutes to complete the form; (3) 35 minutes to assemble and file the application; for a total estimated average of 55 minutes per application. If you have comments regarding the accuracy of this estimate or suggestions for making this form simpler, write to the Bureau of Citizenship and Immigration Services, Regulations and Forms Services Division (HQRFS), 425 I Street, N.W., Room 4034, Washington DC 20529; OMB No. 1615-0013. **Do not mail your completed application to this address.**

U.S. Department of Justice
Immigration and Naturalization Service

OMB No. 1115-0005

Application for Travel Document

START HERE - Please Type or Print

Part 1. Information about you.

Family Name	Given Name	Middle Initial

Address - C/O

Street # and Name		Apt. #

City	State or Province

Country	Zip/Postal Code

Date of birth (month/day/year)	Country of Birth

Social Security #	A #

Part 2. Application Type (check one).

a. ☐ I am a permanent resident or conditional resident of the United States and I am applying for a Reentry Permit.

b. ☐ I now hold U.S. refugee or asylee status and I am applying for a Refugee Travel Document.

c. ☐ I am a permanent resident as a direct result of refugee or asylee status, and am applying for a Refugee Travel Document

d. ☐ I am applying for an Advance Parole to allow me to return to the U.S. after temporary foreign travel.

e. ☐ I am outside the U.S. and am applying for an Advance Parole.

f. ☐ I am applying for an Advance Parole for another person who is outside the U.S. *Give the following information about that person:*

Family Name	Given Name	Middle Initial

Date of birth (month/day/year)	Country of Birth

Foreign Address - C/O

Street # and Name		Apt. #

City	State or Province

Country	Zip/Postal Code

Part 3. Processing Information

Date of Intended departure (Month/Day/Year)	Expected length of trip

Are you, or any person included in this application, now in exclusion or deportation proceedings?
☐ No   ☐ Yes, at (give office name) _____

If applying for an Advance Parole Document, skip to Part 7.

Have you ever been issued a Reentry Permit or Refugee Travel Document?
☐ No   ☐ Yes, (give the following for the last document issued to you)

Date Issued	Disposition (attached, lost, etc)

Continued on back.

FOR INS USE ONLY

Returned	Receipt
_____	
_____	

Resubmitted
_____
_____

Reloc Sent
_____
_____

Reloc Rec'd
_____
_____

☐ Applicant Interviewed on

Document Issued
☐ Reentry Permit
☐ Refugee Travel Document
☐ Single Advance Parole
☐ Multiple Advance Parole
Validity to _____

If Reentry Permit or Refugee Travel Document
☐ Mail to Address in Part 2
☐ Mail to American Consulate
☐ Mail to INS overseas office
AT

Remarks:
☐ Document hand delivered
On _____ By _____

Action Block

To Be Completed by
Attorney or Representative, if any
☐ Fill in Box if G-28 is attached to represent the applicant

VOLAG#

ATTY State License #

Form I-131 (Rev. 10/13/98)N

Part 3. Processing Information. (continued)

Where do you want this travel document sent? (check one)

a. ☐ Address in Part 2. above

b. ☐ American Consulate at (give City and Country, below)

c. ☐ INS overseas office at (give City and Country, below)

    City   Country

If you checked b. or c., above, give your overseas address:

Part 4. Information about the Proposed Travel.

Purpose of trip, *If you need more room, continue on a separate sheet of paper*	List the countries you intend to visit.

Part 5. Complete only if applying for a Reentry Permit.

Since becoming a permanent resident (or during the last five years, whichever is less) how much total time have you spent outside the United States?

☐ less than 6 months   ☐ 2 to 3 years
☐ 6 months to 1 year   ☐ 3 to 4 years
☐ 1 to 2 years   ☐ more than 4 years

Since you became a Permanent Resident, have you ever filed a federal income tax return as a nonresident, or failed to file a federal tax return because you considered yourself to be a nonresident? (If yes, give details on a separate sheet of paper). ☐ Yes   ☐ No

Part 6. Complete only if applying for a Refugee Travel Document.

Country from which you are a refugee or asylee:

If you answer yes to any of the following sheet of paper, explain on a separate sheet of paper.

Do you plan to travel to the above named country? ☐ Yes   ☐ No

Since you were accorded Refugee/Asylee status, have you ever: returned to the above-named country; applied for an/or obtained a national passport, passport renewal, or entry permit into this country; or applied for an/or received any benefit from such country (for example, health insurance benefits)? ☐ Yes   ☐ No

Since being accorded Refugee/Asylee status, have you, by any legal procedure or voluntary act, re-acquired the nationality of the above-named country, acquired a new nationality, or been granted refugee or asylee status in any other country? ☐ Yes   ☐ No

Part 7. Complete only if applying for an Advance Parole.

On a separate sheet of paper, please explain how you qualify for an Advance Parole and what circumstances warrant issuance of Advance Parole. Include copies of any documents you wish considered. (See instructions.)

For how many trips do you intend to use this document? ☐ 1 trip   ☐ More than 1 trip
  If outside the U.S., at right give the U.S. consulate or INS office you wish notified if this application is approved.

Part 8. Signature.   *Read the information on penalties in the instructions before completing this section. You must file this application while in the United States if filing for a reentry permit or refugee travel document.*

I certify under penalty of perjury under the laws of the United States of America that this petition, and the evidence submitted with it, is all true and correct. I authorize the release of any information from my records which the Immigration and Naturalization Service needs to determine eligibility for the benefit I am seeking.

Signature   Date   Daytime Telephone #

Please note: If you do not completely fill out this form, or fail to submit the required documents listed in the instructions, you may not be found eligible for the requested document and this application will have to be denied.

Part 9. Signature of person preparing form if other than above. (sign below)

I declare that I prepared this application at the request of the above person and it is based on all information of which I have knowledge.

Signature   Print Your Name   Date

Firm Name   Daytime Telephone #
and Address

Department of Homeland Security
U.S. Citizenship and Immigration Services

I-693, Report of Medical
Examination and Vaccination Record

START HERE - Please type or print in CAPITAL letters *(Use black ink)*

Part 1. Information about you *(The person requesting a medical examination or vaccinations must complete this part)*

Family Name (Last Name)

Given Name (First Name)

Full Middle Name

Home Address: Street Number and Name

Apt. Number

Gender:
☐ Male   ☐ Female

City

State

Zip Code

Phone # *(Include Area Code) no dashes or ()*

Date of Birth *(mm/dd/yyyy)*   Place of Birth *(City/Town/Village)*   Country of Birth

A-number *(if any)*

U.S. Social Security # *(if any)*

Applicant's Certification

I certify under penalty of perjury under United States law that I am the person who is identified in **Part 1** of this Form I-693, Report of Medical Examination and Vaccination Record, and that the information in **Part 1** of this form is true to the best of my knowledge. I understand the purpose of this medical exam, and I authorize the required tests and procedures to be completed. If it is determined that I willfully misrepresented a material fact or provided false/altered information or documents with regard to my medical exam, I understand that any immigration benefit I derived from this medical exam may be revoked, that I may be removed from the United States, and that I may be subject to civil or criminal penalties.

Signature - Do not sign or date this form until instructed to do so by the civil surgeon

Date *(mm/dd/yyyy)*

Part 2. Medical examination *(The civil surgeon completes this part)*

1.   Examination

Date of First
Examination

Date(s) of Follow-up Examination(s) if Required:

Date of Exam

Date of Exam

Date of Exam

Summary of Overall Findings:

☐ No Class A or Class B Condition   ☐ Class A Conditions (see 2 through 5 below)   ☐ Class B Conditions (see 2 through 6 below)

2.   Communicable Diseases of Public Health Significance

A. Tuberculosis (TB)

☐ Tuberculin Skin Test (TST) (Required for applicants 2 years of age and older: for children under 2 years of age, see pp. 11-12 of Technical Instructions at http://www.cdc.gov/ncidod/dq/civil.htm.)

Date TST Applied

Date TST Read

Size of Reaction *(mm)*

☐ Chest X-Ray - Required **ONLY** for TST reactions of ≥ 5mm or if specific TST exception criteria met, or for an applicant with TB symptoms or immunosuppression (e.g., HIV). **Attach copy of X-Ray Report.**

Date Chest X-Ray
Taken

Date Chest X-Ray
Read

Results
☐ Normal
☐ Abnormal (Describe results in remarks.)

Findings:

☐ No Class A or Class B TB   ☐ Class B1 Pulmonary TB   ☐ Class B2 Pulmonary TB   ☐ Class B, Other Chest
☐ Class A Pulmonary TB Disease   ☐ Class B1 Extra Pulmonary TB   ☐ Class B, Latent TB Infection   Condition (non-TB)

Remarks: (Include any signs or symptoms of TB, additional tests, and therapy given, with stop and start dates and any changes.)

(Family Name)	(First Name)	(Middle Name)	☐ Male ☐ Female	Birth Date (mm/dd/yyyy)	Citizenship/Nationality	File Number A

All Other Names Used (Including names by previous marriages)	City and Country of Birth	U.S. Social Security # (If any)

	Family Name	First Name	Date, City and Country of Birth (If known)	City and Country of Residence
Father				
Mother (Maiden Name)				

Husband or Wife (If none, so state.) Family Name (For wife, give maiden name)	First Name	Birth Date (mm/dd/yyyy)	City and Country of Birth	Date of Marriage	Place of Marriage

Former Husbands or Wives (If none, so state) Family Name (For wife, give maiden name)	First Name	Birth Date (mm/dd/yyyy)	Date and Place of Marriage	Date and Place of Termination of Marriage

Applicant's residence last five years. List present address first.

Street and Number	City	Province or State	Country	From Month	From Year	To Month	To Year
						Present Time	

Applicant's last address outside the United States of more than one year.

Street and Number	City	Province or State	Country	From Month	From Year	To Month	To Year

Applicant's employment last five years. (If none, so state.) List present employment first.

Full Name and Address of Employer	Occupation (Specify)	From Month	From Year	To Month	To Year
				Present Time	

Show below last occupation abroad if not shown above. (Include all information requested above.)

This form is submitted in connection with an application for: ☐ Naturalization ☐ Other (Specify): _____ ☐ Status as Permanent Resident	Signature of Applicant	Date

Submit all copies of this form.	If your native alphabet is in other than Roman letters, write your name in your native alphabet below:

Penalties: Severe penalties are provided by law for knowingly and willfully falsifying or concealing a material fact.

Applicant: Be sure to put your name and Alien Registration Number in the box outlined by heavy border below.

Complete This Box (Family Name)	(Given Name)	(Middle Name)	(Alien Registration Number)

(Family Name)	(First Name)	(Middle Name)	☐ Male ☐ Female	Birth Date (mm/dd/yyyy)	Citizenship/Nationality	File Number A

All Other Names Used (Including names by previous marriages)	City and Country of Birth	U.S. Social Security # *(If any)*

	Family Name	First Name	Date, City and Country of Birth (If known)	City and Country of Residence
Father				
Mother (Maiden Name)				

Husband or Wife (If none, so state.) Family Name (For wife, give maiden name)	First Name	Birth Date (mm/dd/yyyy)	City and Country of Birth	Date of Marriage	Place of Marriage

Former Husbands or Wives (If none, so state) Family Name (For wife, give maiden name)	First Name	Birth Date (mm/dd/yyyy)	Date and Place of Marriage	Date and Place of Termination of Marriage

Applicant's residence last five years. List present address first.

Street and Number	City	Province or State	Country	From		To	
				Month	Year	Month	Year
						Present Time	

Applicant's last address outside the United States of more than one year.

Street and Number	City	Province or State	Country	From		To	
				Month	Year	Month	Year

Applicant's employment last five years. (If none, so state.) List present employment first.

Full Name and Address of Employer	Occupation (Specify)	From		To	
		Month	Year	Month	Year
				Present Time	

Show below last occupation abroad if not shown above. (Include all information requested above.)

This form is submitted in connection with an application for: ☐ Naturalization ☐ Other (Specify): _____ ☐ Status as Permanent Resident	Signature of Applicant	Date

Submit all copies of this form.	If your native alphabet is in other than Roman letters, write your name in your native alphabet below:

Penalties: Severe penalties are provided by law for knowingly and willfully falsifying or concealing a material fact.

Applicant: Be sure to put your name and Alien Registration Number in the box outlined by heavy border below.

Complete This Box (Family Name)	(Given Name)	(Middle Name)	(Alien Registration Number)

(Family Name)	(First Name)	(Middle Name)	☐ Male ☐ Female	Birth Date (mm/dd/yyyy)	Citizenship/Nationality	File Number A

All Other Names Used (Including names by previous marriages)	City and Country of Birth	U.S. Social Security # *(If any)*

	Family Name	First Name	Date, City and Country of Birth (If known)	City and Country of Residence
Father				
Mother (Maiden Name)				

Husband or Wife (If none, so state.) Family Name (For wife, give maiden name)	First Name	Birth Date (mm/dd/yyyy)	City and Country of Birth	Date of Marriage	Place of Marriage

Former Husbands or Wives (If none, so state) Family Name (For wife, give maiden name)	First Name	Birth Date (mm/dd/yyyy)	Date and Place of Marriage	Date and Place of Termination of Marriage

Applicant's residence last five years. List present address first.

Street and Number	City	Province or State	Country	From Month	From Year	To Month	To Year
						Present Time	

Applicant's last address outside the United States of more than one year.

Street and Number	City	Province or State	Country	From Month	From Year	To Month	To Year

Applicant's employment last five years. (If none, so state.) List present employment first.

Full Name and Address of Employer	Occupation (Specify)	From Month	From Year	To Month	To Year
				Present Time	

Show below last occupation abroad if not shown above. (Include all information requested above.)

This form is submitted in connection with an application for: ☐ Naturalization ☐ Other (Specify): _____ ☐ Status as Permanent Resident	Signature of Applicant	Date

Submit all copies of this form.	If your native alphabet is in other than Roman letters, write your name in your native alphabet below:

Penalties: Severe penalties are provided by law for knowingly and willfully falsifying or concealing a material fact.

Applicant: Be sure to put your name and Alien Registration Number in the box outlined by heavy border below.

Complete This Box (Family Name)	(Given Name)	(Middle Name)	(Alien Registration Number)

OMB No. 1615-0008; Exp. 05/31/09

Department of Homeland Security
U.S. Citizenship and Immigration Services

G-325A, Biographic Information

(Family Name)	(First Name)	(Middle Name)	☐ Male ☐ Female	Birth Date (mm/dd/yyyy)	Citizenship/Nationality	File Number A

All Other Names Used (Including names by previous marriages)	City and Country of Birth	U.S. Social Security # *(If any)*

	Family Name	First Name	Date, City and Country of Birth (If known)	City and Country of Residence
Father				
Mother (Maiden Name)				

Husband or Wife (If none, so state.) Family Name (For wife, give maiden name)	First Name	Birth Date (mm/dd/yyyy)	City and Country of Birth	Date of Marriage	Place of Marriage

Former Husbands or Wives (If none, so state) Family Name (For wife, give maiden name)	First Name	Birth Date (mm/dd/yyyy)	Date and Place of Marriage	Date and Place of Termination of Marriage

Applicant's residence last five years. List present address first.

Street and Number	City	Province or State	Country	From Month	Year	To Month	Year
						Present Time	

Applicant's last address outside the United States of more than one year.

Street and Number	City	Province or State	Country	From Month	Year	To Month	Year

Applicant's employment last five years. (If none, so state.) List present employment first.

Full Name and Address of Employer	Occupation (Specify)	From Month	Year	To Month	Year
				Present Time	

Show below last occupation abroad if not shown above. (Include all information requested above.)

This form is submitted in connection with an application for: ☐ Naturalization ☐ Other (Specify): _____ ☐ Status as Permanent Resident	Signature of Applicant	Date

Submit all copies of this form.	If your native alphabet is in other than Roman letters, write your name in your native alphabet below:

Penalties: Severe penalties are provided by law for knowingly and willfully falsifying or concealing a material fact.

Applicant: Be sure to put your name and Alien Registration Number in the box outlined by heavy border below.

Complete This Box (Family Name)	(Given Name)	(Middle Name)	(Alien Registration Number)

Instructions

What Is the Purpose of This Form?

Complete this biographical information form and include it with the application or petition you are submitting to U.S. Citizenship and Immigration Services (USCIS).

USCIS will use the information you provide on this form to process your application or petition. Complete and submit all copies of this form with your petition or application.

If you have any questions on how to complete the form, call our National Customer Service Center at **1-800-375-5283**.

Privacy Act Notice.

We ask for the information on this form and associated evidence to determine if you have established eligibility for the immigration benefit you are seeking. Our legal right to ask for this information is in 8 USC 1101 and 1255. We may provide this information to other Government agencies. Failure to provide this information may delay a final decision or result in denial of your application or petition.

Paperwork Reduction Act Notice.

A person is not required to respond to a collection of information unless it displays a currently valid OMB control number.

We try to create forms and instructions that are accurate, can be easily understood and that impose the least possible burden on you to provide us with information. Often this is difficult because some immigration laws are very complex.

The estimated average time to gather the requested information, complete the form and include it with the appropriate application or petition for filing purposes is 15 minutes. If you have any comments regarding the accuracy of this estimate or suggestions for making this form simpler, write to U.S. Citizenship and Immigration Services, Regulatory Management Division, 111 Massachusetts Avenue, N.W., Washington, D.C. 20529; OMB No. 1615-0008. **Do not send your form to this Washington, D.C. address.**